The Urbana Free Library
To renew: call 217-367-4057
or go to "*urbanafreelibrary.org*"
and select "Renew/Request Items"

More Advance Praise for *Beyond the First Draft*

"In *Beyond the First Draft,* John Casey invites the aspiring writer to sit down for coffee with a wise and sympathetic mentor. These essays will remind you why you love to write and will inspire you to hone your craft further."   —Tom Young

"John Casey is a classroom raconteur: erudite, passionate, fierce, and funny. How fortunate, then, that those who haven't had the opportunity to be his student can now be mentored by him via this collection of emotionally generous and vivid essays on the art of fiction. I tore through the selections, adding my marginal scribbles of surprise and delight. The volume is a treasure, and I will return to it often."   —Pamela Erens

"John Casey is a superb craftsman, a legendary teacher, and an omnivorous reader. The combination makes this book of essays a literary delight. It is pure gold for the young, and not so young, writer trying to master the craft."
—Christopher Tilghman

"A major writer and master teacher, John Casey brings his formidable intellect to bear on the art of fiction. He describes his elusive subject in prose as accessible as conversation only wittier—aphoristic and anecdotal, full of winning confessions of youthful follies in the practice. Casey's wide reading and experience furnish these essays with shrewd exempla, portraits of other writers, their texts, procedures and consequences. *Beyond the First Draft* shimmers with the wonderment of its author for the wonder of fiction." —Christine Schutt

"These practical and provocative craft essays are the next best thing to being in a workshop with the brilliant writer and teacher John Casey—or in his own writing cabin, just after he's settled into the armchair across from you with his French-pressed coffee and a pipe. Personal, insightful, colorfully anecdotal, *Beyond the First Draft* is more than a writing handbook—it's a singular contribution to the conversation about how fiction is made and what it can do." —Eleanor Henderson

Beyond the First Draft

ALSO BY BY JOHN CASEY

Room for Improvement
Compass Rose
The Half-life of Happiness
Supper at the Black Pearl
Spartina
Testimony and Demeanor
An American Romance

TRANSLATED BY JOHN CASEY

Enchantments
You're an Animal, Viskovitz!

John Casey

Beyond the First Draft

THE ART OF FICTION

W. W. Norton & Company

NEW YORK | LONDON

Copyright © 2014 by John Casey

All rights reserved
Printed in the United States of America
First Edition

For information about permission to reproduce selections
from this book,
write to Permissions, W. W. Norton & Company, Inc.,
500 Fifth Avenue, New York, NY 10110

For information about special discounts for bulk purchases,
please contact W. W. Norton Special Sales at
specialsales@wwnorton.com or 800-233-4830

Manufacturing by Courier Westford
Book design by Brooke Koven
Production manager: Julia Druskin

Library of Congress Cataloging-in-Publication Data

Casey, John, 1939–
Beyond the first draft : the art of fiction / John Casey. — First edition.
pages cm
Includes bibliographical references and index.
ISBN 978-0-393-24108-2 (hardcover)
1. Fiction—Authorship. 2. Fiction—Technique. 3. Creative writing.
4. Fiction—History and criticism. I. Title. II. Title: Art of fiction.
PN3355.C295 2014
808.3—dc23
2014021536

W. W. Norton & Company, Inc.
500 Fifth Avenue, New York, N.Y. 10110
www.wwnorton.com

W. W. Norton & Company Ltd.
Castle House, 75/76 Wells Street, London W1T 3QT

1 2 3 4 5 6 7 8 9 0

Contents

Beyond the First Draft

PREAMBLE

THESE ESSAYS aren't the alpha and omega of good advice, but they aren't the ABC's either. Perhaps the first one is. "Dogma and Anti-dogma." They contain some notions of my own and a lot of help from Aristotle to Zola.

Most of them were originally presented as "craft talks" at the Sewanee Writers' Conference over the last twenty years or so. A few of them were answers to specific requests. I've edited and in some cases rewritten them.

I remember Stanley Elkin starting one of his Sewanee craft talks by saying, "It's . . . hard . . . to talk about . . . art." He said this very very slowly. He paused for a while. Because Stanley was a man of many humors, most of them humorous, a few prankish, some people thought that first sentence might be all he was going to say.

I'll bet he was tempted. He certainly milked the pause.

Of course he went on. With that first sentence he wasn't apologizing or asking for indulgence. He was just setting the bar high. And then sailing over it. Crouched in his wheelchair he gave a funny, grouchy, instructive talk.

It's hard to talk about art—so we should all be nervous. It's hard to talk about art—but I've been around the block.

That's Stanley I'm channeling. I'm not so sure I'd put it like that. I'd rather say I've been into the woods a lot. Sometimes I found the trail. Sometimes I lost it. Sometimes I had to spend the night in a pile of dead leaves.

These essays are suggestions about things to do, things to think about, when your writing has got you lost in the woods.

DOGMA AND ANTI-DOGMA

The dogma isn't meant to crush your first draft.
Think of these venerable sayings as hints from Tarot
cards or the I Ching.

A COMMON THING people ask me about writing classes is "Can
you teach someone to write?"

I have two answers.

The first is no . . . but if someone is talented to begin with, I
can save her a lot of time.

The second answer is also no . . . I can't teach someone to
write, but I can sometimes teach someone to rewrite.

For a long time I taught the way I'd been taught. I'd been in
classes taught by Peter Taylor, Kurt Vonnegut, Vance Bourjaily,
José Donoso, and what they did—after you turned in a story—
was to tell you what they thought you'd done. Basically they'd
say, "Here is what all those marks on the pages meant to me."

And then I could figure out if that's what I'd wanted to do—or if there was now something else I could do that looked better.

This holding up the mirror is a good way to be helpful to a beginning writer. Writing a story or a novel is like finding your way around a strange room in the dark. When you get through the first draft you think the light will go on. But it often doesn't. At first you need a reader you can trust to tell you what you've done . . . and that there is or isn't hope for this particular effort.

I think this process is useful because the majority of good beginning writers are at first less in love with structure or pattern and more in love with the *words* in a foolish but sweet way.

I don't think people should skip this sweet foolishness. There is this to be said for it: you are falling deeply in love with language; you are, at last, learning your own language. If the sweetness outweighs the foolishness, if the genuine outweighs the foolishness, if the genuine outweighs the synthetic, if the verbal inventiveness and precision outweigh the clichés of plot and callow characterization, it's a helpful stage. It may be as good for the future as plowing under a field full of oats.

When Katherine Anne Porter taught at the University of Virginia, her method was to sit the student writer down and read his story to him aloud. That's all there was to it, or so I've heard tell. I've also heard that one student, before his story was half read, broke down and ran.

I'm sympathetic. Long ago a kind editor at a Boston publishing house took an interest in my earliest novel. Over lunch he told me, "You have talent, dear boy." I felt for an instant like one of those saints in Italian paintings on whom a beam of divine light falls. He then said, "Of course, some of this writing is . . . embarrassing."

"Oh yeah," I said. "Like what?" (Sometimes you just can't help leading with your chin.)

He opened the manuscript and read aloud.

After a bit I said, "Ahh." Or maybe it was "Arrgh."

He advised me to plow it all under. I did.

Three years later I salvaged a part of a chapter, turned it inside out, and used it in a story, the first piece I sold. (Moral: plow under, but save a copy just in case.)

But the sophomore, the wise fool, the sweet fool, has to be done away with sooner or later. So what comes next?

From the writer's point of view it seems like more of the same: the inspiration, the rise of hope, the realization, on one's own now, that some part of the piece has failed. You've had your hand held, someone has held up a mirror, but now it's time for sterner stuff. Dogma.

Is dogma helpful? Let us hear some:

- "Write for yourself."—J. D. Salinger, or at least one of the Glass boys
- "Write about what you know."—Everybody says this.
- "Above all, I want to make you see."—Joseph Conrad
- "You must tell your story in the fewest words possible."—Sean O'Faolain
- "A short story must have a single mood and every sentence must build toward it."—Edgar Allan Poe
- "Tell the truth."—Everyone again
- "Stalk the billion-footed beast—be a reporter."—Tom Wolfe
- "Conventional narrative bores me; you must experiment."—Robert Coover
- "Culture is local."—William Carlos Williams

There are many other dicta, but these are all at the core. They are also ones I've been told, have told myself, and have told others; frequently they were just what the doctor ordered.

SALINGER'S "WRITE FOR yourself." Yes, there is something wonderful about a writer who has her own voice. And there is something horrible about the sound of an imitated voice. There are writers whose works you can pick up and the particular hum of the prose is immediately recognizable; there is an intimacy your inner ear recognizes even before the rest of your brain approves. This intimacy is not necessarily gentle or nice, but I'm pretty sure that the only way to achieve it is in communion with yourself, a communion that is in some way innocent, however fierce or forgiving.

Of course, the dictum applies to subject matter as well as tone or style. It can be a good prescription for the stylishly voiced but timid. Find the subject that leaves you mute, then tell it.

BUT. If you were to take this dictum as your only course and not a course correction, you could end up on the rocks.

Arthur Koestler, in the second chapter of his autobiography *Arrow in the Blue*, justifies himself and apologizes for autobiography in general. Among his warnings, the chief is against nostalgia.

Twenty years ago I covered a bass-fishing tournament for *True* magazine. The winner of the tournament was a laconic fishing guide from Arkansas. I spent a day with him picking up tips on how to catch fish—the conditions of structure, season, sun, and so on. I asked him at last if there were things to watch out for in all this finding the right spot to fish.

"Nostalgia," he said.

I figured out what he meant. I'd spent hours plugging away

at a stretch of water where I remembered with great pleasure catching a beauty. But if the fish aren't there now, all you catch is nostalgia. Moonbeams of your peculiar unrelatable memory.

BUT. There's another *but*. Kurt Vonnegut used to say to his class at Iowa, "You've got to be a good date for the reader." The rest of the metaphor of courtship could be inferred. Query: Can you bring flowers and write for yourself? Can you wear perfume and write for yourself? As long as it's still you.

But surely you have some friends to whom you would never ever say—just before they set out for a blind date—"Oh, just be yourself."

There is a falsity or pandering one must rid oneself of, but there is often a sincere but boring side too. If I were to go on a blind date, I'm sure that my wife, four daughters, and three sisters would all call out, "For God's sake, don't talk about rowing!"

"Be a good date" can let you be a mere entertainer.

"Write for yourself" can let you be a nostalgic bore.

But in the sense that "write for yourself" is "know yourself," "find your own demon, your own angel," it is the first commandment of useful dogma.

"WRITE ABOUT WHAT you know." An example of this good advice:

I had two students who were writing costume drama. One was writing about Mayan warriors—sacrifice, sex, and slaughter. The other about gentlewomen in Alabama in hoop skirts. Both went on and on. I finally said to each, "Stop."

The woman who'd been going on about hoop skirts, said, "What shall I write about then?"

"Talk to me a bit, tell me what you know."

She said, "I see you're looking at my knee." This was back in the first round of miniskirts. She went on, "See how it doesn't quite fit? It's going to make me lame unless I have an operation, but I have had a phobia of hospitals ever since I was strapped to a gurney when I was little. It was a Labor Day weekend and the room was full of people screaming, I was there for hours, days, I can still hear them whenever I smell that hospital smell . . . whenever I smell that hospital smell I get migraines so bad I can't see, literally, can't see . . . ."

I said, "Come back in two weeks with seven pages about your knee."

She wrote a five-page piece called "Patella" that was riveting. It was, in the apt phrase of my first wife, "hysterically calm." It won the $500 prize for the best short story at the University of Virginia.

So I told the man the same thing. Write a five-page story about something closer to you than Mayan slaughter. He came back with a wonderfully condensed piece about a man sitting at Mass (about a quarter of the writing was simply the words of the Mass). There was a woman next to him. Her sleeve brushed his sleeve. He concentrated on prayer. Her shoulder brushed his. Was she doing it on purpose? Was she sick? Fainting?

They stood for the Gospel. He wouldn't let himself look at her. He only saw the hem of her raincoat when they sat down. He listened to her breathe. He tried to concentrate on the sermon.

I don't remember how it ended. It was abrupt, I think. *Ite, missa est.* Go, the Mass is ended. He (the character) was still caught in uncertainty; he'd half resisted the temptation, half succumbed . . . if the temptation was really there. He was freed by the fact that he could never possibly recognize her, never find out what she'd meant. Perhaps there was some regret.

I thought how much more full of conjured sensuality, of tension, of a real psyche and spirit this piece was than all the hundred and fifty pages of exotic Mayan sex and slaughter.

"Write about what you know" . . . could there be any *buts*? Two occur to me. Suppose Leo Tolstoy had decided to end *The Death of Ivan Ilych* before Ivan Ilych is dying and has a vision—because Tolstoy didn't really know what dying is. One answer is that Tolstoy imagined it so vividly that he *did* know. Gustave Flaubert imagined the death agony of Madame Bovary so intensely that he vomited. Perhaps the best version of this dogma for some people is "Write about what you know, but move into that rich intertidal zone between the dry beach of what you know and the sea of what you don't."

Rudyard Kipling wrote wonderful stories about the Indian army. He'd hung out with soldiers when he was a reporter in India. Later, when he'd become famous and was living in England, the Royal Navy made him an honorary officer and asked him to come on training cruises. He got royal tours of the ships—the engine room, the bridge, the officer's ward room, and so on. Kipling was an inquisitive man and a quick study. He used his navy material, but the navy stories are lifeless. They are filled with navy lingo and detail, but they don't live. What is the moral of this experience? It may be that if you acquire technical knowledge quickly, without the slower sense of the emotional forces carried by these *things* in a communal life, you will prattle. Even if you are Kipling. Perhaps the qualifying dictum is this: he who learns a little soon repeats it. Kipling had some of his best work still ahead of him, from "They" (1904), "The Wish House" (1924), and on into the thirties. I love stories about writers with rich autumnal years.

CONRAD'S "ABOVE ALL, I want to make you see" is a wonderful motto. Fiction often fails because it isn't visible enough. I see my own early bad writing repeated year after year by otherwise gifted young writers because they want to get right to the metaphysics. But when they or I get to what things look like—not just picturesque landscapes but people's expressions, light on water, the way a worker works—things perk up.

Ernest Hemingway had a motto similar to Conrad's. It's more or less this: write about what people do, what people say, and what the weather is like. Cyril Connolly in his wonderful and odd book *The Unquiet Grave* gives Hemingway his due for having succeeded in awakening the readers' senses.

But the real wonder of fiction is that it not only appeals to the senses—it makes all of your shadow senses receive the world of the story—but also at its very best it gives us a sixth sense, a sense of the invisible forces that make people more than the sum of their five senses. Conrad, though he is the author of the motto, certainly conjured the invisible as well as the visible. As writers, you do finally have to conjure, whether by implication or direct statement, invisible forces as specifically as you have conjured a bullfight, a bank robbery, a kiss. Consider the end of *The Great Gatsby*. The end of *The Sun Also Rises*. All of *Nostromo*.

So perhaps we can amend Conrad and say, "First of all, I want to make you see." If you can do that then you can go on, then you have earned the right to the invisible.

"YOU MUST TELL your story in the fewest words possible." The book in which Sean O'Faolain says this, *The Short Story*, is one of the few useful works on the subject. It is one-half anthology, one-half commentary.

I can't explain why shortness is a good thing. I can only think of how many gallons of maple sap it takes to make one gallon of maple syrup—forty. Maple sap tastes like water—very good water, but water. Maple syrup is a miracle.

Sean O'Faolain doesn't mean that you must tell simple stories that begin with the beginning, go through a middle, and stop at the end. Supreme examples of rigorous cutting and condensations are Isaac Babel's *Red Cavalry* and Muriel Spark's *The Girls of Slender Means*.

I believed this dictum even before I read it. It was in the babbling gossip of the air. The first story I sold was one I condensed. For ten evenings I more or less copied the handwritten pages of the third and what I thought was the final draft onto new pages, and at the end of each evening, I would count with satisfaction, "There: four pages into three." Next time—"There: six pages into four and a half."

Reading aloud helps. You can feel the places where the density isn't what it should be. Reading aloud to prepare a piece for reading aloud in public helps even more. You tend to ask yourself, "Do all those people need to know all of this?"

BUT. Even here there is a *but.* Sean O'Faolain tries to demonstrate how Henry James's long story "The Real Thing" can be cut. He puts brackets around the unnecessary parts. He was brave enough to pick a story by a master. It's a very close call whether he has improved the James story. My students have split about fifty-fifty on this question.

My own further experience is odd. My first published novel, *An American Romance*, was 604 pages in typescript when I sent it to my agent and to my editor. They both said, "Way too long. Make it shorter."

I worked for six or seven months. There were 100 pages on the floor of my workroom when I finished. I did write a few little additions. I typed it up again. It came to 640 pages. What the hell. I sent it in.

My agent and my editor wrote back independently of each other, "Good. It's much shorter."

An Italian fencing master I once knew used to ask his students, "How does the frog catch the fly? Because he is quickest? No! Because he has *tempo*!"

Tempo, timing, pace, rhythm. The shortest distance between two points is a frog's tongue. Thank you, maestro.

"A SHORT STORY must have a single mood . . ." Poe went on to say that every sentence must contribute to it. He wrote this in a review of Nathaniel Hawthorne's stories, saying that Hawthorne brilliantly fulfilled this requirement of unity and coherence. So do a lot of Poe stories. The dictum is a terrific idea, one I'd guess he came to from his reading and writing lyric poetry. It is a short-story writer's alternative to the suggestions about unity made by Aristotle for tragedy.

Both Poe and Aristotle are trying to be helpful in this quest for unity. But what's so hot about unity?

I can't explain unity any more than I did brevity. In *The Biology of Art*, Desmond Morris writes that certain apes and a few monkeys produce paintings that show an instinctual urge toward both symmetry and unity. It is a fascinating book with lots of beautiful pictures, particularly some by chimpanzees (Picasso owned a picture by Congo, the star chimp artist); I also like the delicate spirals turned out by the capuchin monkeys, and some of the work by Sophie, a gorilla who would paint only when she was separated from her mate.

Kurt Vonnegut has a nice sentence about yearning for unity—and brevity too—in *Slaughterhouse-Five*. The beings of Tralfamadore, a distant planet, have novels; each is a single dot that fits on your fingertip and, when applied to your forehead, zaps you with the essence of the novel.

My own daydream of unity could have been the Parthenon, the Pantheon, or a well-wrought urn, but at the particular right moment I happened to see a catboat on her cradle. Her lines defined her perfectly yet didn't seem to be limits. Every line curved toward another but didn't end when it met the other. All the lines seemed endless continuations of each other, an endless continuation of the whole. She was a single idea that looked enormous in a neat way but also as if you could pick her up in the palm of your hand.

Virginia Woolf describes a character in *The Years* having a physical experience of architecture. Considering a building, she (the character) feels weights move inside her until (I may be making up this part) on their own they find the balance the building has. It is possible to read some buildings in that way: standing in the center or sensing their center from outside, you feel their balance so enormously but so wholly that you imagine you could extend your fingertips to every part.

Are there stories or novels like that? One of the pleasures of the days following reading *Pride and Prejudice, Moby-Dick, Madame Bovary*—and many others—or stories like Nikolai Gogol's "Overcoat" and its descendant, Frank O'Connor's "Guests of the Nation," is that sensation of feeling the lines moving out and around and back through the whole.

Could there be any *buts* about the unity that Poe or Aristotle, each in his own way, wish for us?

There *are* buildings like the one in Virginia Woolf's *The Years*, like the Pantheon and its descendants by Andrea Palladio and Thomas Jefferson. Yet there are others like that in which the prince in Giuseppe di Lampedusa's *The Leopard* lives. As I remember it, he thinks that it would be boring to live in a house in which you knew all the rooms. I imagine his house as a history of Sicily—each century adding another piece in its own style with lots of accidental spaces caught inside like air bubbles in amber.

There are novels like that: old ones, perhaps *Don Quixote*, and at least one new one, Graham Swift's *Waterland*. And I can think of one wonderful story: Alice Munro's "Oranges and Apples," which starts in a mood or mode of chronicle of provincial life but turns into something else and something else again: larva, chrysalis, imago. The last instar something so gorgeous you could never have guessed it from the first pages.

Would Aristotle or Poe have helped her? But that doesn't mean that they're not helpful to her or the rest of us on the many occasions of pondering what to do with the jumble of incidents and tones that we're trying to rewrite.

Perhaps these pieces of dogma are like saints for different perplexities: Saint Antony of Padua for finding lost things, Saint Blaise for curing sore throats, Saint Christopher for traveling safely (though I hear he's been displaced, alas).

EVERYONE SAYS "TELL the truth." But I have in mind Konstantin Stanislavski.

I used to assign and still suggest Stanislavski's *An Actor Prepares* to my writing classes. There are two main reasons. Stanislavski gives a good argument against cliché. If you use a cliché in your preparation for a role, you put a roadblock in front of any further imagining. Clichés are vague, large, inert, and therefore terminal. The other reason is less a warning, more a positive aid. If a character in fiction is lifeless, it often helps for the writer to play the part. Do all the preparation Stanislavski asks an actor to do. Imagine the character's life offstage. What does she eat? How? What does she fear? How does she dress? How does she feel going home? Et cetera, et cetera. Out of this imagining will come a hundred details, and usually one of them will provide a life-giving drop.

I had an odd experience with the narrator of a long story of mine called "Connaissance des Arts." He was an okay guy but was neither hot nor cold. Perhaps I was afraid someone would think he was me. So I changed his clothes, put him in a good suit and a custom-made striped shirt with a white collar. I gave him narrow feet and put good shoes on them. I didn't need to mention any of this in the story. He began to act differently. The gulf that he perceived between him and his favorite student at the University of Iowa became more painful for him, at the same time his feelings for her became sharper. I don't know if the story is good, but it became more alive.

An Actor Prepares is a simply written series of lessons at a rhetorical level of *Dick and Jane*'s "See Spot run." It is a work of genius. But . . . I sometimes have misgivings about it. One is that Stanislavski didn't have a great sense of humor. Anton Chekhov kept writing him, when Stanislavski was directing Chekhov's plays: "Please, Konstantin, it's meant to be funny." The other misgiving is that Stanislavski seems to hold that the memory of one fear, for example, can animate the fear of the character to be portrayed. You might, relying only on your own emotions, inflate your jealousy at your junior high prom into Othello's. There is a danger of using emotions as isotopes or platonic ideals. It can work; I have only a misgiving about this, not an objection.

The antidote to this last misgiving about Stanislavski's method, as valuable a tool as it often is, can be found in the work of another Russian, Vladimir Nabokov, specifically in *Speak, Memory*. Among the many things *Speak, Memory* is, it is a manual on the art of memory. Nabokov's memories are not interchangeable, although he could bestow them on certain of his characters as dangerous gifts. They are conjured for themselves, in all their infinite particularity. It is infinite particularity that is Nabokov's argument against cliché.

There is a wonderful chapter on his drawing teachers. Without deploying his whole pattern of development, from the facile and sweet to the labored and expressionistic to the precisely observed and rendered (so precise was Nabokov's observation and rendering that he was once employed by Harvard's Peabody Museum to do drawings of butterfly genitalia!), I'll simply characterize that chapter as perfect miniature commentary on the dialectic (how he would grind his teeth at that word) of becoming an artist, whether visual or verbal.

So there are at least two saints in this tell-the-truth niche. Tell the truth, implore the intercession of one saint or the other or both, and tell it again. A tenor in an Italian town was called back for a third encore. "Thank you, thank you," he said. "But I can't . . ." A voice from the crowd called out, "You'll sing it again until you get it right!"

TOM WOLFE'S DOGMA: "Be a reporter." Here's an easy one, but it comes up frequently enough to be worthwhile. Wolfe wrote an essay in *Harper's* magazine in 1989 on how to write a novel. In essence it said, "Go out and be a reporter. The material is out there! Get out of your ivory tower, stick a pencil stub behind your ear and do it the old-fashioned way. You could be Balzac, you could be Zola, you could be me!" There are some writers you'd like to see kicked in the pants in just this way.

I read a very good book (now out of print) several years ago:

Nimrod of the Sea by William Morris Davis, a story of American whalemen. Every reportorial detail that is in *Moby-Dick* is in there, and then some. In addition to harpooning, a Nantucket sleigh ride, the tryworks, and so on, there are icebergs in the Bering Sea, surfing in Hawaii, and a wealth of other lore. But *Nimrod of the Sea* is no *Moby-Dick*.

I like *Nimrod of the Sea*. It should be reprinted. But still, a first-rate way to learn the difference between very good reporting and the art of the novel is to read both books.

"CONVENTIONAL NARRATIVE BORES me." Robert Coover then went on to say, "You must experiment."

He was one of the smartest teachers at the University of Iowa when I was there. At that time it looked as if he, along with John Barth, would be the North American answer to Jorge Luis Borges. It could still work out that way.

Both Coover and Barth appear in a dozen, no, a score, of recent anthologies of short fiction. Their best stories are wonderful. The best of Barth is probably "Lost in the Fun House." It *is* experimental. It plays with language, with received ideas, with the convention of narrative, with the architecture of the fun house and the architecture of the very fiction we are reading. There is a host of Barth works on which the same descriptive label could be pinned. Some are good, some are sterile. All the smart stuff is there, but it's solving a chess problem.

I think the qualification of the command to experiment is this: variation for variation's sake, experiment for experiment's sake, are for the notepad, for the sketchbook. Experiments work in art when they contain the same emotional charge that good fiction always has. Originality is not a sufficient condition for

storytelling. When the experiment is attempted as a way to produce a charged state of being, so that less of the charge is lost in
transmission, *then* you're trying for the big gold ring.

"CULTURE IS LOCAL." William Carlos Williams was a pal
of Ezra Pound. Ezra Pound whirled off to England and Italy,
learned Latin, Italian, Provençal, and delighted in Chinese
poems. His allegiance, his literary allegiance, was European. In
ABC of Reading, a rich swath-cutting primer with a great reading
list, Pound says intimidatingly that if you want to know poetry
and don't know Latin and Provençal, you might still have some
fun in English. He's not an antiquarian—he's in favor of writers
who've brilliantly upset the applecart—but he harks back and
abroad.

William Carlos Williams stayed home. He did do a young
man's European tour, but then he set up in New Jersey and practiced medicine, wrote about Paterson, his patients, his home
ground.

I like teaching Williams's *The Farmers' Daughters* because in
those prose pieces he does find what is wonderful down the
street, around the corner. There are famous stories in it—"The
Use of Force," "The Girl with the Pimply Face"—but my favorite is "Old Doc Rivers," the life of an old-time country doctor,
with a kind of genius and a terrible restlessness. (*The Farmers'
Daughters* is also reassuring to students because some of the stories are great successes and some are instructive duds.)

Once again we have two patron saints. Do they cancel each
other out? Is it an either/or?

I was wandering around Washington, DC, one day, wonder-
ing why there's so little good fiction written about it. The good
American political novels are set elsewhere. *All the King's Men* is

set in Louisiana; other good political fiction comes from Boston or Chicago. (There's a little bit of good stuff about journalism—a subculture that is local in the sense of sealed in and centripetal.) It occurred to me that politicians, like most TV shows, are trying to write themselves as broadly appealing, and they end up as clichés. But then at my feet I saw another answer. In front of the National Theatre there's a plaza on whose paving stones are inscribed quotations about Washington. The one on which I was standing said, "Washington—neither Rome nor home."

I wish I'd said that. (When Oscar Wilde wistfully murmured that he wished he'd said a smart wisecrack he'd just heard, James Whistler said to him, "You will, Oscar, you will.")

Washington, so far at least, hasn't been a matrix for either the Pounds or the William Carlos Williamses. (One footnote exception comes to mind, a good book of stories—*Lost in the City* by Edward P. Jones—which is set in Washington, but it is about black Washington, a population by and large excluded from the national media nonculture, but with a William Carlos Williams culture of its own.)

As to our two saints—Pound of Rome and Williams of home—there's another way of setting up the difference. It is the distinction between the tale and the modern short story. A tale occurs when someone leaves home, goes over the hills and far away, and comes back to tell the folks what amazing things are out there. A short story occurs when someone stays home and ponders local life until she can produce what is amazing about the things going on in her own culture, in her own words. Both the tale and the short story can be all the things our first eight points and counterpoints of dogma exhort us to write.

After considering these exhortations and their undertows, are we back where we started? Nobody thought that when you are facing the imperfect, half-alive matter you have committed to the page, that you could dial 1-800-OUR-DOGMA. As so often happens in law, the question isn't just what the laws are but which ones apply to the case. Writing fiction—rewriting fiction—is trial and error, intuition and amended intuition. But in the effort to find your way through your own material, an application of one or another of these suggestions from our inherited lore may provide the right course correction.

IF I WERE A FLOWER,

WHAT KIND OF FLOWER WOULD I BE?

A suggestion about how to suggest changes to a manuscript without invasive surgery.

I N THE 1960s the requirements for the master of fine arts degree in creative writing at the University of Iowa Writers' Workshop included two courses of "another art." The most popular choices were music (playing an instrument), life drawing (a prerequisite for painting), and film (unlimited use of an 8 mm camera and all the film you could shoot for a small lab fee; NO sound).

Why this requirement for another art?

I think it was because those other arts have disciplines that can be isolated technically when learning the ABC's. Learning to write prose fiction is a muddle, because, among other things, language is as much a constant of our life as air. Around us and inside us. Moreover, the impulses and technique of narrative are, if not inherent in language, at least intertwined with our learning language in the first place. When my oldest daughter was two, I'd get back from work and say, "What did you do today?" She would narrate lunch—"bread . . . and peas . . . and"—a tedious but thrilling-to-Dad chronology of food or toys. But one day, when I said, "So how was your day?" she hesitated a long while. Then she said, "A dragon came. A dragon came and flew all around." I would have been pleased with this invention except she said it with great pain. It turned out she had been tormenting her baby sister and her mother hit the roof. My older daughter moved from learning how to chat to composing fiction.

Consider by contrast some arts that are narrative but exclude language. Silent movies, ballet, modern dance, mime. Even opera, since for American audiences the language is usually just part of the sound. All these are enormously stylized. Gestures and expressions are exaggerated, rendered into a kind of hieroglyphics. In silent film, for example, there are the leer and mustache twirl of the villain; the averted face and fraily out-thrust arm of the heroine; the arriving hero in profile, square jaw jutting, manly chest like the prow of a ship. Shortly thereafter, the villain's slinking away in hunched contraposto and the maiden's clasping her hands at her breast in prayerful gratitude. A ridiculous and lovable set of masks and postures—occasionally used with inspiration and elegance—but at a distance, the distance of conventional artifice. The silent actors, dancers, and mimes translate themselves into Egyptian hieroglyphics, and we have the pleasure of reading this language which is as formal, familiar, *and* alien to us as Latin used to be for Catholics at Mass.

To present a story in this way you have to learn the ABC's of the discipline before you get up onstage or on-screen. You can learn dance (years of pliés and battements at the barre). You can learn to sing (years of scales and exercises to achieve pear-shaped tones). You can go to clown college (acrobatics, pratfalls and the many venerable things to do with slapsticks and seltzer bottles). There might be differences of opinion about details but no confusion about the rudiments.

In pictorial or plastic arts each discipline has its physical materials whose properties must be learned. And then exercises and lessons for the different levels of neophyte, apprentice, and master. Whether considering sculpture, painting, or architecture, very few people imagine they can just do it.

Like most people, I've had to learn how to do a number of things both for business and pleasure. Business and pleasure is one way to divide them. Another is to separate them into those things that have a defined academy and those that are just part of living. I took lessons in Latin grammar, law, basic military training, and so on. In middle age, tap-dancing, judo, sculling. I've watched four daughters learn gymnastics, horseback riding, lacrosse, piano, cello, and fiddle. I've also seen the two older children evolve as published writers, each in her own particular and mysterious way. Our instructors in sports and other arts had a lot of ABC's to set forth. By contrast, what I had to say to my writing daughters was tentative, gnomic, fragile, and usually metaphorical.

When you submit to formal instruction in most crafts or arts, you go through the schoolroom door and disencumber yourself of passions for a while. You bring your passions back later on, when your technique is strong enough to bear them. Story writing is closer to being one of those things that just happens in life, like falling in love, marrying, child rearing, or friendship. You're in the midst of it before you know what you're doing.

An old law professor of mine said, "When you practice law you're living in the vortex of other people's passions." When you're creating a story from what you've felt, seen, heard, or dreamed, you're in the vortex not just of other people's passion but also your own. Perhaps it's truer to say you're alternating between being tumbled in the ring of turbulence and being poised in the vortex. But still surrounded by turbulence.

Perhaps it was a sense of that situation that made the Iowa MFA chiefs require the study of another art. They may have given up trying to start their instruction with a formal initiation and decided instead to send the MFA candidates through the door of a neighboring schoolhouse and let the drawing masters and piano teachers shrive the students. Perhaps the hope was that the students would then become more patient— less frustratedly ambitious, more patiently ambitious. In a field where they felt less anxiety they might learn the dispassion that must precede the representation of passion. (And yes, there must be passion again. There is a dialectic: initial passion, dispassion, passion. Let's stipulate that dispassion can be the absence of passion, a postponement, a displacement, or a vortex inside passion.)

The MFA chiefs may have also had this thought: while literary criticism as practiced in English departments provides a vocabulary of appreciation or analysis for readers, it's not very good at helping writers. It tends to be an occasion for psychoanalysis, sociology, history, linguistics, or politics rather than an adoption of Aristotle's stance in his *Poetics*, which I take to be "You playwrights and other writers have given me great pleasure, so I'd like to suggest how you might give me even more." So the MFA boffins may have thought that if they sent their students off to other arts that *do* have vocabularies of instruction, those vocabularies could be invoked as analogies. "Look. Remember what you learned about perspective in drawing class? Well, maybe your story needs a vanishing point."

As often happens with a good poetic idea when it becomes

administrative policy, this one didn't work out, at least not in a determinate way.

One of my housemates already played the piano very well, and he was happy to sign up for instruction and to play even better, without, I think, drawing any instructive parallels to his writing. Another of my housemates took a life-drawing class, the chief result of which was that he took up with two of the models, one in the fall, another in the spring.

I myself wandered over to an audition in the singing division of the Music Department. I imagined a small room with a piano and some nice person playing a chord and asking me to sing the notes. Instead I found myself being ushered onto the stage of a theater. The first rows of the audience were filled with sopranos in silk blouses holding opera scores. A jury of faculty members sat in the last row. One of them asked me in a beautifully carrying baritone to give my sheet music to the pianist. Sheet music? I picked singing because I thought it was one of the life things. Like walking and talking.

I said to the pianist, "Do you know 'The Bonnie Earl O'Murray'?" He shook his head disdainfully.

Baritone from the rear: "Are you sure you're in the right place?"

I explained the other-art requirement of the Writers' Workshop. The baritone hadn't heard of it. He said, "It takes years of training to produce pear-shaped tones. Our students go on to professional careers. But go ahead and sing your little ditty."

I sang. The baritone said, "Sing it higher." I began again. The baritone interrupted. "That's the same note." I went rashly higher. Luckily the heat of embarrassment loosened my voice instead of strangling it. Perhaps there was some heat of anger too.

The baritone turned to the other faculty. "Anyone willing to take this one on . . . for his 'other art'?" A woman said yes, but the baritone spoiled it by asking me if I could sight read. "Before we let you take up this good lady's time, you must take a semester of piano. Otherwise you won't be able to do your homework, will you?" The proposition was reasonable, however infuriating his tone.

I said no. I regret this now. I wish I could have ignored the baritone and learned to make pear-shaped tones for the good lady in the back row. But perhaps it was as well to have a little rebellion. I'd been through basic training, been berated by sergeants. I'd been through law school. Two of my first-year professors were rumored to have been models for the acidic Professor Kingsfield in *The Paper Chase*. Yet another professor addressed his first-year class on the first day: "Some of you are here to become lawyers so you'll be powerful and/or rich. I have no interest in you. Others of you are here because you want to reform society, to be engineers of social progress. You are less venal but equally uninteresting. A very few of you may have the intelligence to become mandarins. It is to you that I will be saying anything of value."

I'd been through all that. I'd crossed the Mississippi to reach the free territories.

I filed a brief to that effect with the assistant administrator of the Writers' Workshop. He read it and said, "You don't want to do it? Okay. So what'll I write in the blank space? Army or law? The art of army sounds kind of dumb. Let's say law."

I'd come in truculent. His easy okay wrong-footed me. That moment of being off-balance helps keep the question from being filed away: what can be prescribed in the education of a writer?

The memoirs of English and North American writers that I've read suggest that their vocations were both fated and accidental. Vladimir Nabokov is a brightly contrasting intrusion into our culture. In *Speak, Memory* he tells us that while he was at Cambridge he worked his way through a three-volume Russian etymological dictionary, mastering the roots (and flowers) of his first language. There is another chapter in *Speak, Memory* about his three drawing masters and his three-stage progress: (1) delighting in easy effects, (2) confusion, and (3) mastery of detail. It is explicitly helpful about drawing, implicitly about writing. Most North American writers' memoirs are about encounters with life rather than about programs of artistic training. Ernest Hemingway didn't acknowledge, let alone describe, Gertrude Stein's tutoring him. And in general, he said, you shouldn't talk about writing: if you do, you risk spoiling it. Perhaps a lot of North American writers take Ishmael's remark about his education to be Herman Melville's: "A whale-ship was my Yale College and my Harvard."

We love our writers who just up and write American. Mark Twain, of course, Walt Whitman's barbaric yawp, Hemingway—particularly in a story like "Light of the World"—J. D. Salinger giving voice to Holden Caulfield, Nelson Algren.

I remember a group class at Iowa led by Vance Bourjaily and Nelson Algren. When called on for comment, I compared the student story under discussion to a cello suite: "Her long mournful sentences . . . the way she bows some of those phrases . . ." Algren cut in. "Okay. Okay—you like it." General laughter. I was dancing around with too big a lead, got picked off at first.

Other apprentices apparently felt more seriously aggrieved. In another class held by Kurt Vonnegut someone asked what was up with Algren, Algren was going around saying that he thought his job at Iowa was to discourage as many people as possible. Where does he get off saying stuff like that? Vonnegut thought a bit and quoted, I think from memory, a paragraph from *Notes from a Sea Diary: Hemingway All the Way*, a late nonfiction book by Algren. Algren describes going ashore in an Indian port, Calcutta as I recall. A beggar woman approaches him. She is rail thin, covered with sores. Maybe her baby is starving—I don't remember all the details. I do remember the last two sentences. "I gave her a nickel. I would have made it a dime but I didn't want to corrupt her."

A few people in the front row twisted back in their chairs, just an inch or two. What kind of man would . . . ? But most people got it, sooner or later—Algren's feeling is compressed and coded into that wisecrack. An American version of a Zen koan.

So what was Vonnegut saying to us? Or not saying? Aside from "Listen to this," he may have been saying, "If Algren tastes like vinegar, he probably feels like vinegar. He's been around the block. He's not talking much, but you could pick up a thing or two."

José Donoso taught a Marcel Proust seminar. Each class hour one of us seminarians would present a paper. Donoso would listen to it and then listen to our comments, registering shades of interest or boredom on his beautiful bearded face. Then he'd get a brainstorm. The one I remember most vividly was to this effect: "You Anglo-Saxons, you North Americans must remember that Proust is French. That is, closer to being Latin. That is, delighting in smells and tastes of all kinds. Not just the nice smells. Not just the pretty smells. Smells of decay, of rot. If you will open your senses, you will open your imaginations."

Donoso could do the standard items—French society, the Dreyfus affair, World War I (yes, yes, part of Proust is in its way a war novel)—but his provocative extravagant homilies were vital.

Robert Coover scared me. I thought, not entirely wrongly, that he stood for the annihilation of received ideas—and conventions and plots. I also admired his reconfiguring of what he deconstructed (that word wasn't in the literary vocabulary then—Coover was ahead of the times). Part of his aesthetic was like that of F. T. Marinetti's "Futurist Manifesto" for artists in the Europe of the 1920s: Blow up the museums . . . A speeding car is more beautiful than the Winged Victory of Samothrace. I think I took that aspect of Coover too literally. "Hey, wait, don't blow that one up. I haven't read it yet." Another aspect of Coover's approach (as I gleaned it from his students and from his work) was the requirement for a chess player's planning. I didn't want to have such a totally conscious dialogue with whatever demon of storytelling was in me.

I do wish that I had taken Coover's seminar on Cervantes.

Vance Bourjaily was the one who really lived in Iowa. He gave me companionable and practical advice while introducing me to fields, woods, and creeks. We also worked on a political campaign together. He was young and generous in his enthusiasms (hunting, pig roasts and parties, dogs, jazz), interested in and knowledgeable about how the worldly world works, and understated but clear about how all this interest and fun is at no safe distance from misfortune.

But how did they talk to us about our writing? It wasn't ABC's. Vonnegut said to me about one of my early stories, a bit of lyricism set in a Swiss boarding school, "It's perfume. Perfume, perfume, perfume." Maybe I should have showed it to Donoso who might have had an idea about how to put a life-giving drop of ambergris in it. And then again maybe it was just as well that I got to fret by myself.

Vonnegut's remark about a much better story (later to be my first sale) was more encouraging. "I like the way the narrator comes on stage, the way he says to the audience, 'You know me.'" Of course the narrator/character doesn't actually say any such thing, but I knew what Vonnegut meant. At last I was playing a character who had a life, who had enough of a real life that he could step on stage and get right down to it. I wasn't *writing*, the bane of decent writing, as *acting* is the bane of decent acting.

And, as it happened, acting had been my "other art." I'd acted a lot in college. By accident I'd discovered that I didn't stutter on stage. (That accident is another story . . .) It occurs to me now that stuttering is in its turn a good preparation for acting. When I was in a period of stuttering badly, I was locked in silence. So I spent a lot of time imagining conversations. A kind of never-ending *espirit d'escalier.* Acting is in one way the opposite of silence, but in another way it is a vow of silence except for those words the play blows through you as if you are one pipe of an organ. Several schools of acting suggest that an actress imagine in detail what her character has been doing for the hour or day or life before she enters. Or that an actor write out a subtext to his lines, a stream of consciousness that won't be uttered but that will color what he says aloud. All that locked-in imagining should make the character true, or at least truer. I learned *about* that lesson, but I didn't really learn it until late in the game. My senior year in college I got to play Cardinal Monticelso in John Webster's "The White Devil." Webster in sensibility is somewhere in between his contemporary William Shakespeare (especially where Italian plots and counterplots come in) and our own morbid Edgar Allan Poe. Example: Duke Bracciano, who is in love with Vittoria the white devil, is married to a wife so doting that she kisses his portrait each night. Bracciano smears the portrait's lips with poison. He gets the poison from a doctor, "a poor quack-salving knave . . . he will poison a kiss and was once minded, for his masterpiece, because Ireland breeds no poison, to have prepared a deadly vapor in a Spaniard's fart that should have poisoned all Dublin." It's a terrific play—exuberant both in its low comic relief and its high villainy. The director was a playwright who'd adapted *Billy Budd* for Broadway. The actress playing the title role was one of two or three professionals in the big roles. She was an Englishwoman with definite manners and style. She and I had a ten-page trial scene at the end of which I ordered her locked up. After we'd been in rehearsal for a couple of weeks she took me to an empty room and said something like this: "I want to go higher in that scene. I can't, unless you do too. Tomorrow we'll come back here and do the scene. I want to feel you trying to destroy me. Surely it couldn't be for mere crime. Perhaps you, Cardinal Monticelso, desire me. I'm married to your lout of a nephew and I'm making love to Bracciano. Didn't you try out for that part? I wonder what . . . But you're that beastly priest, Cardinal Monticelso."

I was twenty-two. She was a glamorous older woman, perhaps twenty-nine or thirty.

The first part of what she said to me—about building the scene—was good advice. The second part, the taunting flick of her whip, should have worked—would have worked—if I hadn't been more scared of her than up to feeling manly desire. What I felt was that I'd been coolly teased, then dazzled. One good thing that came out of it was that I so wanted to please her that I worked very hard and at least started to come back at her with enough energy and pace for her to build on. Her notion of bracing my priestly role with sublimated lust didn't pan out, but our private sessions worked in other ways. I kept on being scared of her, but also, after a while, I saw that she was doing all this not so much out of comradely goodwill but to make herself shine. I began to feel some rivalry, and that was enough to get me to respond to her person-to-person as opposed to playing against her role as I'd merely read it on the page. When we began to rehearse in costume I saw that she looked smashing, but I was engaged enough in my part to live in my cardinal's robes, to menace her in her beautifully fitted white gown with my own scarlet vehemence.

I never played the cardinal, or any part, as well as I would have liked. But there was this lesson: you study basic principles, you listen to advice, but then you have to do something with your own hands. Do it over and over until the discipline and advice and the written lines are all part of the dirt you're getting dirty in. To which you must add some part of your living self, some reflex that snaps *now*.

I don't know. I don't know if I did that. I don't know if she and I ever gave off the cold fire that the playwright stored up in the lines.

> CARDINAL: Who knows not how when several night by
> night
> Her gates were chok'd with coaches, and her rooms
> Outbrav'd the stars with several kind of lights;
> When she did counterfeit a prince's court
> In music, banquets and most riotous surfeits?
> This whore, forsooth was holy.
> VITTORIA: Ha! Whore! What's that?
> CARDINAL: Shall I expound whore to you? Sure I shall;
> I'll give their perfect character. They are first,
> Sweet-meats which rot the eater; in man's nostril
> Poison'd perfumes . . .

and so forth for twenty-one more lines of scarlet hiss and outrage, to which Vittoria says:

> VITTORIA: . . . For your names
> Of whore and murdress they proceed from you,
> As if a man should spit against the wind;
> The filth returns in's face.

The reason the cardinal goes on about the lights, music and feasting—innocent enough to modern urban sensibilities—is

that Vittoria's carryings-on violated sumptuary laws, which reg-
ulated what food, clothes, and other display different classes were
entitled to. The phrase "did counterfeit a prince's court" gives
a sense of the cardinal's sense of the wrong. His lurid "whore"
rant probably owes something to the Malleus Maleficarum, a
witch-hunter's handbook of 1484: "[W]hat else is woman but a
foe to friendship, an unescapable punishment . . . a delectable
detriment, an evil of nature painted with fair colors!"

All that is of literary and historic interest, early preparation
for the part. The more difficult stage followed. That is, did we
make any of that true on stage? With our mouthfuls of blank
verse, our fear, vanities, stage fights—the whole folderol of putting on a play—did we bring John Webster alive?

I think we may have if for no other reason than that I can still
hear her voice, feel her as a bitter enemy, feel the air between us
thickening with her anger and contempt.

So when Kurt Vonnegut spoke to me in terms of theater, we
understood each other. His remarks encouraged and reassured
me that my story cycle of first-person narrators could draw on
the bit of theater discipline I'd taken in as audience, assistant
director, and actor.

This notion of writing fiction as some sort of method acting
can be set against what I understand to be the Gordon Lish
notion of writing as bravura performance. First let me say that
the Lish school must have had some good influence. At least five
writers I know went through his seminar: Lily Tuck, author of
Interviewing Matisse, a brilliant comic dialogue; Mark Richard,
author of *The Ice at the Bottom of the World*, stories with fairy-tale
drastic clarity; Amy Hempel, a writer of stories that start as snap-
shots and become x-rays; and Yannick Murphy, author of *The
Sea of Trees*, a prison camp novel that is as beautifully refracted as
J. G. Ballard's *Empire of the Sun*; and Christine Schutt, whose *All*

Souls is masterful. And there are many more authors who speak of Lish gratefully and admiringly. But here is a piece of Lish advice that I think is dangerous: Write a sentence that knocks the socks off the reader. Make the next sentence more exciting. And so on.

What I think is dangerous is that this can make the writer the equivalent of a stand-up comic. So what's wrong with that? I find most stand-up comics tediously assaultive (one exception being Paula Poundstone). Stand-up comics aren't creating a sustained character or narrative. They're trying to shoot lines that will jump-start the target audience's nervous reflexes. The comic doesn't treat the audience as people like him but as a subspecies of underlings to be jolted into response, jazzed up, jerked this way and that. It's bull fighting or lion taming—human tricks to control animal response. It's not an invitation to approach a representation of life as a sentient, intelligent, and imaginative equal of the performer. It's sock 'em with this, then hit 'em with that.

The analogy holds for story writing. I've seen many stories ruined by the writer's going for a low laugh line (a particularly American failing) or show-off wit or toniness (Brits) or other prodding attempts to impress the reader. I'm not against laughs or elegance—all for 'em, provided they don't break the surface tension of belief in the story, a surface tension on which both the performer/writer and the audience/reader are poised like water striders.

Like water striders . . . Like . . . As if . . .

Some analogies are specific and point for point. When I was in the army, I saw two recruits trying to learn how to tie their neckties. They were off the farm for the first time and so shy that instruction, especially in alien accents, confused them. A sergeant who happened to be from somewhere like their homeplace

saw the problem and said, "It's just like you tie a mule halter."
That was that.

Some analogies require more from the speaker and listener.
In her book *The Body in Pain*, Elaine Scarry writes that analogies
are the only language a sufferer has. The patient can only say
things like "It's as if someone's sticking a needle . . ." or "As if
there were a red hot coal . . ." or "Like a drill . . ."

Scarry quotes Virginia Woolf: "[T]he merest schoolgirl when
she falls in love has Shakespeare or Keats to speak her mind for
her, but let a sufferer try to describe a pain in his head and language at once runs dry."

So what do you do when language runs dry?

Scarry gives a flicker of hope.

This is not to say that one encounters no variations in the inex-
pressibility of pain as one moves across different languages.
The existence of culturally stipulated response to pain—for
example, the tendency of one population to vocalize cries, the
tendency of another to suppress them—is well-documented
in anthropological research. So too a particular constellation
of sound or words that make it possible to register alterations
in the felt experience of pain in one language may have no
equivalent in a second language: thus Sophocles's Philoctetes
utters a cascade of changing cries and shrieks that in the original Greek are accommodated by an array of formal words
(some of them twelve syllables long) but that . . . one translator
found could only be rendered in English by the uniform syl-
lable "Ah" followed by variations in punctuation ("Ah! Ah!!").

I wanted to hear a word like that. I asked the chair of the
Classics Department at the University of Virginia to help me
find it. She read me the scene in which Philoctetes screams. (He

is suffering from a suppurating wound in his foot caused by a snakebite. Because it stinks and because he won't shut up about it, the Greeks maroon him on an island for nine years. They come back to get him because only *he* and his bow can defeat Troy. When they find him he's still suffering.) He cries out, "A a a a." And then, "Papai, apappapai, papa papa papa apai." And at last, "Pappapappapai." Five or five and a half syllables. I was still hopeful. I asked what *pappapappapai* means. Alas, nothing formal. Something like "arrgh" or "aiee," the sort of cries I remember from DC Comics. Scarry needn't have bent over backward in her argument. I was disappointed. But I'd checked the book out of the library so I reread the facing-page translation of the play. There *were* more powerful indications of pain. Philoctetes asks Neoptolemus to take his sword and cut off his heel. "Lop it off quickly! Do not spare my life." Or, in another translation, "Strike the end of my foot. Strike it off." However awkward the wording, the intensity comes through. Anyone suffering for a night with a bad toothache has said to a dentist in the morning, "Pull it out. Just pull the damn thing out!" The measures one will go to find relief are a measure.

A few lines later Philoctetes says something that I find even more evocative, more expressive—perhaps not so much of the intensity of physical pain as of the anxiety of pain. One translator has Philoctetes speak of a spasm that has come on him as a female personage. "She comes from time to time, perhaps when she has had her fill of wandering in other places." The literal translator writes, "It has come in person after a time, perhaps because it is weary of wandering, the sickness." Whatever the gender, the notion of pain as a banshee who flits away for no apparent reason and then swoops back gives another dimension. It is a bit of imagining squeezed out of Philoctetes as if it were a drop of cold sweat on his forehead or the ooze of his unhealing wound.

Scarry is right to be stopped short in front of the blank wall of formal language, of single specifying words. But as in the case of Philoctetes, that wall can be breached or skirted both by a narrative context and by analogy. Scarry's initial proposition is right enough—a gloss on the ancient adage "No one can feel another's pain." But the idea that pain is a unique case of the inexpressible I find unconvincing. There are lots of experiences—of pleasure as well as of pain, of gloom as well as grace—that lack an ABC of direct language. I'm reminded of a line by Donald Justice: "As if . . . but everything there is is that." (That line puzzled me until I read it out loud with a pause between the first and second *is*.)

I'm grateful for the struggle with Scarry's propositions for a couple of reasons. The first is that they got me thinking of the power of "as if" rather than its paucity. The second is that I was reminded of the general dread of being isolated in any experience that one cannot describe to another person. It is a dread that sometimes comes as a feeling of being lost in space. Other times it comes as a feeling of being entombed. It is a dread that underlies the effort of storytelling. Suppose the reasonable and sensitive reader on whom one has pinned one's hopes says, "I don't get it. I just don't get it." It can feel as if you're whirled away, tumbling past Uranus and Pluto, or as if your thought and voice are a dwindling speck sliding down into a hole that is caving in.

Hal in *2001* was a malevolent computer, and it was scary enough. But I think the frustration of being isolated on a space station with a computer that knew only Webster's definition and syntax and was indifferent to the intuitions of analogy would be a worse torture. No laughs for one thing. For another, it wouldn't understand your stories.

The game from which I took the title of this essay is called (I think) analogies. The game is played like this: one person is

It. *It* leaves the room and the other players think of a person—a famous person or someone all the players know. *It* comes back and tries to guess. The form of the game is that *It* is the person, so the questions that *It* asks are in the first person: "If I were a flower, what kind of flower would I be? If I were a car . . . If I were a piece of music . . . If I were an animal . . . If I were a country . . . If I were a shoe . . . ?"

What's amazing is that *It* often wins. Since the game isn't competitive but cooperative, the guessing works. The rules allow for *some* elaboration. If *It* is Marilyn Monroe, the answer to "What flower would I be?" might be a peony or a rose or a tulip but could also include some mention of how full blown the blossom.

If *It* were Nixon, someone might say that the flower would be artificial. (If you're *It*, you may have to gauge the sensibilities of the answerer. And I guess it's fair to look at the expressions on the faces of the other people too: dubious frowns or raised eyebrows; an agreeably cocked head.) Nobody who's *It* guesses after just one round. I can't remember how many rounds it usually takes or what percentage of the time it works. I do remember that the game works sometimes. And that the best players either answer that question right away or after a very long time. It isn't a game you can play with your computer.

Talking to another writer about her story eventually calls on skills very like those needed to play "Analogies." You may start by using standard critical terms about pace or point of view or plot, but those are broad-brush notions, especially if the story is pretty good and you're trying to suggest ways to make it better. The first thing is to let the writer know that you have understood it—not just the events but the spirit. A lot of very good writers I've asked for help have responded by telling me a short analogous story, either true or fictitious. This may seem digressive, but it is an efficient form of comment. It has the additional advantage of not intruding.

If the mentor suggests a specific detail to be inserted, it is more often disruptive than helpful. It is as if a director read an actor's line to him and said, "That's how it should sound." A pretty good story already has its own immune system and is likely to reject foreign bodies.

This is not to say that the whole conversation can't get tough. I remember telling a writer that the pace of a particular scene was agonizingly slow. The writer said, "Well, there's a lot I want to get in." I said, "You have enough in. What it's like now is watching at an archery range while someone picks up an arrow and walks to the target and tries to shove it in by hand. You've pulled the bowstring back in the scenes before. Shoot the arrow."

A common fault among younger writers, especially good ones, is to become enchanted with complex ornamentation. They may have seen it in Joyce or Nabokov or Faulkner or Cormac McCarthy. I once took such a writer to the Washington National Cathedral (a good duplication of English gothic). We looked at the vaulting—finer and finer tendrils sprouted. But the bases were as big as a house. You can't see all the way around. You can feel, you can almost hear them, as if you were in the engine room of a ship larger than any ever built. You don't need to explain that you couldn't get the tendrils way up there without these roots. Or that the delicate tendrils wouldn't be as beautiful if they weren't a culmination of force.

Another reason to use analogies of this sort is that they're more apt to incite physical energy. A flow of physical energy is as necessary as efficiency in prose fiction. It may burst or it may be confined. I remember singing in a chorus. A Mozart *Te Deum.* The conductor stopped us. He said, "Okay, so you're right. This passage is marked pianissimo. But in this Mozart I want you to feel it fortissimo and have it come out pianissimo." I sort of got it. Years later I was looking at a stream in Vermont. The snow was melting and the stream was swollen. It tumbled down hard into a pool that seemed to hold the water quietly before letting it out through a fast-running sluice between two boulders. A whole uprooted pine tree came bounding downstream, riding over the white standing waves. It came to rest in the pool, where it floated as lightly as a dry fly. Its black branches and green needles spread out on the shimmer of dark water. Then suddenly it was engulfed. Pulled straight down. I blinked. The tree popped up again in the pool. The branches were ripped away, the trunk half stripped of its bark. It rolled once, showing more white pulp than bark. It drifted out of the pool, slow at first, then riding the faster current between the rocks.

That's what the conductor meant. Not the mangling of the pine tree, but the apparent serenity of the pool, the power at work under the surface.

Although I learned that lesson too late for *Te Deum*, it may surface somewhere else. If not for me, for someone else. I can imagine an actor playing Othello. He enters Desdemona's bedchamber, snuffs out a candle, and strangles her. His line is "Put out the light, and then put out the light." Perhaps he enters on the last part of the fast current of his jealous rage, angrily swiping at the candle with his hand—put out the light. Could the second part of the line—"and then put out the light"—be the dark pool? I do think Othello has had his fortissimo of rage before he enters the bedchamber and the killing is done in a terrible pianissimo.

Having started out with puzzlement at why the Iowa Writers' Workshop once required two courses in another art, I now find myself being swept toward a unified-field theory of the arts. As they used to say in law school when argument began to get too far aloft, "This is getting metaphysical."

On a practical level I find theater the most immediately useful analogy to fiction. A writer will sometimes present a story full of well-imagined characters with good voices, but they're running around too disjointedly. It helps to suggest to the writer that she be a director.

Or a writer presents a story that is orderly but with the characters being marionetted into their plot roles. Or—a less extreme case—one minor character who is lifeless. It helps to ask the writer to play that part—to imagine a day or days in that character's life, not to enlarge the part but to find among the fifty or a hundred reimagined details the one or two that will make that character live. To that end I've sometimes asked writers to read Konstantin Stanislavski's *An Actor Prepares*. It is not a work of art as is Nabokov's *Speak, Memory*, but it has an equivalent courage in daring to examine and instruct the imagination. I'm particularly fond of one of the first exercises. The director asks each member of the class to imagine he or she has lost a diamond stickpin somewhere onstage, perhaps on the floor, perhaps caught in the rear curtain. One by one they act. They run this way and that way, posing in attitudes of search. Just as the last student sits down, a girl comes in late. The director says something to the effect of "In the theater we are on time. You may remain in the class if you find a diamond stickpin that I lost somewhere on the stage." She looks for the pin. She inches her way across the stage. Perhaps she lifts the hem of the curtain and sweeps her fingers along the floor.

The director says to the class, "That's it."

A student objects. "But she's not acting. She's simply looking for the pin."

The director says again, "That's it."

It's a trick. Her anxiety, her directness, her clumsiness and frustration, were given to her. It's truth onstage made simple for her. Can she do it on her own? Can the others? Can they achieve it when they are called on to present greater actions and feelings? Chapter by chapter they learn. First actions, then speech as action. Can writers learn from their learning? Certainly not everything about writing but at least part of the rigor of imagining. If not imagining the truth, at least imagining truthfully.

I sometimes wonder if our stories are already composed in some form or other and that the writing is a performance. The story may be like those short outlines pinned to a board backstage for the improvising players of the *commedia dell'arte* just before they go on as Scaramouche or Columbine or Harlequin, and we have to hope our anxiety, like theirs, will turn to live foolery and wit and action.

Other times I wonder if the story is on one side of the Rosetta stone in a language we don't know. We decipher it slowly. There are images that baffle us. It may be that on the other faces of the stone there are other arts about which we have an inkling. On one face perhaps an art with structural necessities, like architecture. Another face has a fragment of an art that suggests tonality and rhythm, like music or film. The fourth face has a clue from the theatrical art of finding a detail to make a character alive.

I've been analogizing out of my experience; others may have quite different Rosetta stones. My *our* and *we* may be less communal than I hope. My Stanislavski or my Scaramouche may be too particular. But at some time you may need some way to look at what you're working on, some way to consider the parts and the whole, and you may find your field temporarily barren in spite of having worked it as hard as you can. You may find some help in looking at your neighbor's field to see what to do with your own.

JUSTICE

What does justice have to do with story writing? It's as crucial as stresses and strains are to constructing a building.

SOMETIMES JUSTICE is easy: There's just the two of us. You and I have our eye on the piece of cake. I say, "You cut, I choose."

How readily comprehensible that system is, how perfectly symmetrical, how self-contained, how portable through space and time wherever there are conflicting desires, communication, and reason.

Perhaps you would prefer to flip a coin? That's fair, in the sense of equal opportunity, but the symmetry lasts only as long as the coin is in the air. It takes a wonderfully metaphysical loser to be satisfied with savoring the vanished chance while the winner has had her equal opportunity and is eating it too.

There are more instances and more theories than I would

dare to explore, even when dealing with divvying up desserts. What I'd like to get to however, is this: Whatever instances or theories of justice we're working with, there is—even before an invocation of a rule or rules—an imaginative process. And this imaginative process is one that has a great deal in common with the imaginative process that is useful in making up a good story. It requires an adversarial imagination. To be a good adversary, you have to figure out what you want and what the other person wants. Wanting, needing, and claiming for yourself require less imagination.

When I first started teaching fiction writing at the University of Virginia, I happened to get a spate of love stories from my students—forlorn and aggrieved love stories. If the writer was a *he,* the story was she-done-him-wrong. If the writer was a *she,* it was the other way around. These stories had something else in common: they were far too long.

As much by way of self-defense as by way of considered aesthetics, I started asking him to rewrite his story from her point of view, and her from his. All the rewritten stories were much shorter and much more interesting. Several of them even became good.

"Stresses and strains," my old high school English teacher used to say. "It's all stresses and strains." By which he meant writing is construction, is engineering, and that buildings and compositions stay upright by pushes equaling pulls.

Was it push equaling pull that made these stories better? The push of the lyric self-lament (sometimes in the original draft thinly veiled in the third person, sometimes full-frontal first person) was still the initiating force of the story, but in the revised version the push was checked hard by the pull of the other point of view, so that the rewritten story, although *assigned* to be *entirely* from the other point of view, came out balanced. The strategies the students applied were various. Some wrote he-said/she-said versions. Some *did* write from the other point of view but managed to undermine, at least partially, the laments and justifications of the other.

I filed this away in my mind as a version of the FCC equal-time doctrine. I thought this was a clearer and easier slogan than my English teacher's somewhat gnomic "stresses and strains." I now think I may have been careless. The equal-time doctrine accounts for the increased fairness, in the allotted airtime, in the students' stories, but not for the stories becoming shorter and better. I now think that stresses and strains—some sort of conflict, competition, ordeal, or at least adversary proceeding—are helpful elements in the art of fiction.

Another English teacher of mine, in a lecture on James Joyce's *Portrait of the Artist as a Young Man,* pointed out that *Portrait of the Artist* is organized into three parts: lyric, dramatic, and epic. In the lyric stage the protagonist is trying to determine his identity and the boundaries of his identity: what is him and what is not him. The point of view is single. At first it is swaddled in a cocoon. Even when encountering the world, the self is the subject and everything else is other. Everything else is an object of desire or a hostile force or a backdrop to the emergence and growth of the self. For the dramatic stage of literature to come into being, a lyric self must recognize that there is at least one other self populating this universe of everything else, another self capable of similar desires, feelings, and communication. The desires of the other may conflict with those of the protagonist or at least overlap, and the story is now concerned with that conflict as much as with the development of self. The dramatic is not necessarily a higher or better stage. The lyric can be intense, deep, and coherent, as in Proust. Marcel—the primary self if you put aside the interstitial story of Swann—sends out his senses like a swarm of bees, and they gather so much of France, of nature, and of civilization that in the end Marcel has filled his hive with overflowing combs of honey.

Nor is the epic, which won't detain us long, necessarily a higher or better stage. A short definition of an epic is a story in which the fate of the protagonist is coterminous with the fate of his or her tribe or nation: Aeneas leads the defeated Trojans on a voyage and ends up starting Rome. The end of the *Portrait of the Artist as a Young Man* is mock epic: "I go now to encounter for the millionth time the reality of experience and to forge in the smithy of my soul the uncreated conscience of my race." (I confess that when I first read that sentence as a young man I was especially thrilled. I didn't get the mock part. The title of the work is quite rightly *Portrait of the Artist as a Young Man*.)

But you don't necessarily get to choose, and often the dramatic story is thrust upon you. So back to the dramatic. In law school I took a seminar called Theories of Justice. One of the early notions was that a person can't have a concept of justice until she or he recognizes that there are other beings endowed with a capacity for feeling, desire, communication, and reason. This preliminary condition is the same as that necessary for dramatic literature, with the addition of reason.

Aristotle says, "Among friends, there is no justice." By which he means that if you love your friend, you wish for her all good things, whereas justice is concerned with dividing up good things when two or more people want them and good things are in short supply.

About halfway into *Splendeurs et misères des courtisanes* (*A Harlot High and Low*), Honoré de Balzac, writing at his usual headlong pace, found that two of his main characters, a man and a woman, had fallen in love and were living happily in a cozy house in an ideal setting. So he wrote this remarkable sentence: "The history of happiness is boring, so we shall skip the next five years." And with a stroke of his pen, he flung the pair of them back into the perilous currents of Parisian intrigue.

Suppose Balzac is right. Do we hunger after conflict in our reading as much as we hunger after justice in life?

There are some people—and some parts of most of us—that do hunger after a story with sharp edges, in literature and in life. This hunger can take unpleasant forms—for instance, voyeurism or schadenfreude. We even sometimes watch trials as a mob. One of the justifications for criminal trials is that we have to do something by way of retribution or we would *act* as a mob. Better a judicial process that gives the people their day in court. So we may watch a trial hoping to see a villain punished, both by the spectacle and by the sentence. And there is a literature that panders to this: *Death Wish* starring Charles Bronson, superhero stories, and patriotic war films. But there is a more important way that we take in both trials and stories. A story that troubled me in Sunday school was the one about King Solomon and the two women, each of whom claimed a baby. King Solomon heard their arguments, both of which were plausible. King Solomon's advisers were no help. King Solomon then said, "Since we can't decide, we'll divide the baby between you—by cutting it in half." The one true mother shrieked and told Solomon to give the baby to the other woman. The troublesome part comes from sympathy for the mother who believes Solomon. For an instant he uses his royal and judicial power to put her on the rack. And then he makes it all right.

So he's okay. But it isn't his story that interests me. The question that interests me is this: Is the mother worse off by reason of pain and suffering than before she got into this story? Or is she just the same in the end, the law having "made her whole"? Or is she better off?

One aftermath of the story I imagine goes something like

this: Her screaming "No!" and then saying that the other woman should take her child opened her up to a larger love for her child. And perhaps she felt herself larger and stronger and proud of her instincts—fulfilled as much by them as by the decision of the court.

The point I'm after here is that the vise of the dramatic contest, of the judicial proceeding, brought the mother to a perfected state of herself and to a perfected utterance.

I FIND MYSELF shocked by this reasoned praise of agony. Is it too mandarin? Or only too mandarin a way of speaking of an event if it were real life? Is it okay if I'm just taking a connoisseur's approach to a made-up story?

I'm trying to draw on my notions of law and adversary proceedings and use them to learn something about what purpose they serve in fiction. But, as often happened in law school, I tend to linger over the possibilities of the case as story rather than the story as case.

The next question: is contest by itself a good thing? When you start out writing either scripts or stories and you ask an old hand to read them, one of the things that almost always gets said is "But where's the conflict?" And I've been suggesting here that that's a good thing to ask. But there's more to it than that. As I stated earlier, the precondition of a notion of justice is that at least two beings in the world recognize each other as having similar capacities for feeling, desire, communication, and reason.

Another way of saying that someone has a capacity for reason is to say that someone is sane. In our legal system we don't enforce contracts with insane people; we don't punish them for crimes if they don't know what they're doing and can't tell right from wrong. In some ways this is merciful. In some ways it is harsh—by excluding someone from justice we exclude her from humanity. There can still be a struggle, but it's only for control in the sense of dealing with a stray dog. Not quite—we don't kill insane people if they're unclaimed or unadopted after a week at the SPCA. Which, by the way, was what the Nazis did. They cut off food deliveries to insane asylums, a policy consonant with their more general theory of who was human and who was sub-human. But we do deprive insane people of most general legal intercourse, both its responsibilities and possibilities.

And, in a similar manner, we don't generally find them useful as adversaries in stories. (There is an important exception: there is an adversary proceeding in our legal system to determine insanity, and there are good stories—sometimes lyric, sometimes dramatic—of a person's efforts either to regain sanity or to enlarge our notion of who is insane.)

I used to decree to my writing students that they shouldn't use drugs, drink, dreams, or delirium as a way of opening up a character in a story. The good students could always point to good stories that use one of the four devices. The good writers could write good stories that did. But in general I think there is both a loss of compression and a loss of focus in dramatic stories when one of the main characters loses a capacity to recognize the other as similar, and I think that loss is a component of delirium. And what interests me both about justice and drama is not just the recognition of similarity but also that the adversary proceedings usually result in some acknowledgment. Some aspects of our own characters are hidden, either from others or from ourselves, or both. We are often insufficient in ourselves to find our full measure of vice or virtue, or, something that is perhaps more important, what Richard Rorty calls our "final vocabulary." He means by that not just a person's terminology but also a person's sense of things, notions of what values one values most.

Why couldn't perilous adventure serve the same purpose? The hero pitted against the sea, a mountain, a monster. To some extent it does. There are stresses and strains. There is a contest. But what is lacking is the reflective quality, the sense that one adversary is a mirror of the other, even if distorted.

One way to illustrate this point is to consider ghost stories. Most ghost stories have a simple plot. It's "boo!" The ghost is a disaster force like a tornado. One exception to this is a Henry James story called "The Jolly Corner." It starts in an almost infuriatingly leisurely and finicky way. The hero had left New York years before. Resisting family pressure to become a businessman, he went to Europe and tried to become civilized. He now finds New York more hectic, coarse, and combative than when he left. He has returned because he has inherited a house that he always loved. But soon enough we realize that the house is haunted. It is haunted by a more interesting ghost than the usual chain-clanking specter. It is haunted by himself, by the self he would have become had he not gone off to Europe. It is himself endowed with power and shrewdness but devoid of sensibility and cultured intimacy. The hero has to acknowledge that this monster is part of him, that he is not simply a creature of his sojourn in civilized Europe, that there are energies in himself that are fierce and even dangerous, and that he will have to bend them into his life.

One of the most helpful criticisms I've received came from my eldest daughter, herself a writer. She read a rough draft of the eight hundred or so pages of a novel I'd been working on. It is in part about family life. She seemed to accept the representations of conflict as fair and the three points of view as carrying more or less equal weight. All the main characters take their lumps, both from events and from critiques by the other characters. There was equal time; there were symmetrical stresses and strains. Yet she thought something was missing from the main male character.

She said, "He doesn't acknowledge . . ."

I said, "Acknowledge what?"

She said, "Acknowledge enough."

That was just right at the time. Another question that I have is whether acknowledgment is part of the outcome of justice/drama or part of the process. I'm now thinking of acknowledgment as owning up. To answer this question, we have to consider whether we think that pressure can make people tell the truth. I think not. But I think a person under pressure, with no possibility of evasion, can be made to show something that gives a clue. When Solomon put pressure on the mother, she uttered what amounts to a lie, but her verbal act and her demeanor allowed Solomon to guess the truth.

I was once called as a witness at a child custody hearing. Testifying at a trial can be a frustrating, frightening, and brutal experience. It is not just taking an oath administered by the state or standing up to speak in the face of members of your community. There is, under cross-examination, a severe restriction on how much you can say, how much you can explain. The sensation is very like being strapped down on an operating table and being dissected, and the dissector is not someone who is operating for your benefit. What you've said on direct examination is repeated back to you in rearranged and truncated phrasing, sometimes repeated back to you in a tone of sneering disbelief. You tend to forget that the opposing slate of witnesses are going to go through the same thing. You tend to forget that there is any help available from the lawyer who called you or from the judge. You certainly don't think that this cross-examiner, this officer of the court, is playing fair with your honest testimony.

Afterward, you feel humiliated. You feel you've been revealed as nervous, awkward, unconvincing, blundering, irresolute, confused, and weak. You wish you'd been bolder, stronger, louder—a regular Patrick Henry. And you haven't even been on trial; you've only been a witness.

What's the point? What has this degrading adversarial experience to do with truth or justice? The hopeful answer is this: that you have been pressed hard, and all your awkwardness, quavering, and faltering will be understood as the demeanor of a normal person under stress. Perhaps more—perhaps the finder of fact, whether judge or jury, will be able to read more from your unveiled demeanor than you could have conveyed in words alone. It is conventional wisdom that lawyers make lousy witnesses. They foresee the maneuverings of the cross-examiner and can step back and cover themselves. They can come out without a scratch. And nothing comes of it, except perhaps a suspicion that something has been concealed.

All this may be optimistic as regards the operation of justice in our legal system. There are lots of ways in which the process can go wrong. Among other things, it depends on alert, disinterested, and humanely intuitive finders of fact (the sort of people a writer would like as readers). And that takes us back to the comparison of the practice of justice and the practice of story writing.

I'm not saying that you need a formal setting for the cross-examination of your fictional characters or even that the cross-examination be included in the final presentation of the story—just that anytime a character is rolling along unchecked by any other character's wishes, either the writer as director or the writer in the role of another character should set up an impediment that may correct for one side getting to be the only ones we recognize and care for as similar to ourselves.

Shakespeare is full of such moments. The plainest ones occur when a despised character turns on one or more of the privileged characters. An example of this occurs in *The Merchant of Venice*. Shylock is the villain of the comedy. When proposing the terms of his loan—the famous pound of flesh as guarantee—he pretends it's just a joke. He's as much as saying that there's no forfeiture at all because what good is a pound of Antonio's flesh? But near the end, when he has the chance to enforce it, he is the utter villain of the melodramatic portion of the play. Portia, in her capacity as judge, appears to decide in Shylock's favor.

> PORTIA: [to Antonio] Therefore lay bare your bosom.
> SHYLOCK: Ay, his breast.
>> So says the bond; doth it not,
>> noble judge?
>> "Nearest his heart"—those are
>> the very words.
> PORTIA: It is so. Are there balance here to weigh the
>> flesh?
> SHYLOCK: I have them ready.
> PORTIA: Have by some surgeon, Shylock, on your
>> charge
>> To stop his wounds, lest he do bleed to
>> death.
> SHYLOCK: Is it so nominated in the bond?
> PORTIA: It is not so expressed, but what of that?
>> 'Twere good you do so much for charity.
> SHYLOCK: I cannot find it. 'Tis not in the bond.

So at the beginning of the play Shylock is guileful, and near the end so devoid of humanity that his sensibility is shriveled and brittled to the size and stiffness of a clause in his contract.

Only in the middle of the play do we sense him as human, and that in his answer to a question from a gentleman of Venice who asks, "If he forfeit, thou wilt not take his flesh: What's that good for?"

> SHYLOCK: To bait fish withal. If it feed nothing else, it
> will feed my revenge. He hath disgraced me,
> and hindered me half a million; laughed at my
> losses, mocked at my gains, scorned my na-
> tion, thwarted my bargains, cooled my
> friends, heated mine enemies, and what's his
> reason? I am a Jew. Hath not a Jew eyes? Hath
> not a Jew hands, organs, dimensions, senses,
> affections, passions; fed with the same food,
> hurt with the same weapons, subject to the
> same diseases, healed by the same means,
> warmed and cooled by the same winter and
> summer as a Christian is? If you prick us do
> we not bleed? If you tickle us do we not
> laugh? If you poison us do we not die? And if
> you wrong us shall we not revenge? If we are
> like you in the rest, we will resemble you in
> that. If a Jew wrong a Christian, what is his
> humility? Revenge. If a Christian wrong a
> Jew, what should his sufferance be by Christian
> example? Why, revenge. The villainy you
> teach me I will execute, and it shall go hard
> but I will better the instruction.

The general modern readership and audience tend to remem-ber this famous speech as a plea for tolerance: "If you prick us do we not bleed?" But it is more angry and defiant than that.

Shylock lists the ways in which Antonio has wronged him, and when he says, "I am just like you," he isn't saying "I am just like you, so be nicer to me." He's saying, "I'm just like you, and what would you do? You've taught me by your example. Revenge." It's not a speech that asks for recognition of the similarity of *virtues* between the Venetian Christians and Jews: it's more like Charles Baudelaire's demand for recognition: *hypocrite lecteur, mon semblable, mon frère.* Mirror acknowledgment for good or ill.

I wish Shakespeare had written Shylock as more of an antagonist and less a villain, but you can't have everything. *The Merchant of Venice* is a comedy, and in comedy the characters, classically, are worse than we are. The point is that Shylock is given his moment of defiance, and it is his defiance that stands the play upright and makes us glimpse a similar soul rather than an automaton running on the fuel of a single humor. This was a world in which the kings of several European countries, including England, had alternately borrowed money from their Jewish subjects and expelled them.

It was also an old world that was beginning to colonize the new. There was some question among the Europeans about whether the inhabitants of this brave new world had souls—which is to say, were they human?

In *The Tempest* there is a scene early on in which Prospero summons Caliban.

> PROSPERO: Thou poisonous slave, got by the devil himself
>   upon thy wicked dam, come forth.

They put a few curses on each other, and then Caliban reminds Prospero (and us) of their original relationship.

> CALIBAN: This island's mine by Sycorax my mother,
>   Which thou tak'st from me! When thou

>   cam'st first
> Thou strok'st me and made much of me,
> would'st give me
> Water with berries in't, and teach me how
> To name the bigger light and how the less,
> That burn by day and night; and then I lov'd
> thee
> And showed thee all the qualities o'th' isle,
> The fresh springs, brine-pits, barren places
> and fertile—
> Curs'd be I that did so! All the charms
> Of Sycorax, toads, beetles, bats, light on
> you;
> For I am all the subjects that you have,
> Which first was mine own king, and here
> you sty me
> In this hard rock, whiles you do keep from me
> The rest o'th' island.

It's a good brief for an enslaved Adam. In the next exchange, however, Caliban is named villain and confesses to it.

> PROSPERO: Thou most lying slave,
>   Whom stripes may move, not kindness! I
>   have used thee,
>   Filth as thou art, with human care and
>   lodged thee
>   In mine own cell, till thou didst seek to violate
>   The honour of my child.
> CALIBAN: O ho! O ho! Would't had been done!
>   Thou dids't prevent me; I had peopled else
>   This isle with Calibans.

MIRANDA: Abhorrèd slave,
> Which any print of goodness wilt not take,
> Being capable of all ill! I pitied thee,
> Took pains to make thee speak, taught thee
> each hour
> One thing or other. When thou didst not,
> savage,
> Know thine own meaning, but wouldst
> gabble like
> A thing most brutish, I endowed thy
> purposes
> With words that made them known. But thy
> vile race,
> Though thou didst learn, had that in't
> which good natures
> Could not abide to be with; therefore wast
> thou
> Deservedly confined into this rock,
> Who hadst deserved more than a prison.

CALIBAN: You taught me language and my profit on't
> Is I know how to curse.

After this brave defiance—"I had peopled else / This isle with Calibans" and "You taught me language, and my profit on't / Is I know how to curse"—Caliban is shuffled off into the comic relief with Trinculo and Stephano, a couple of sots whom he mistakes for his saviors. In the very end Caliban gets to be part of the general amnesty Prospero declares.

PROSPERO: Go, sirrah, to my cell.
> Take with you your companions. As you look
> To have my pardon, trim it handsomely.

> CALIBAN: Ay, that I will and I'll be wise hereafter
> And seek for grace. What a thrice-double ass
> Was I to take this drunkard for a god,
> And worship this dull fool.

I wonder what happens after Prospero leaves the island, having given up his magic powers and regained his title to Milan. Does Caliban get his island back? You could stage it so that it appears so—Caliban romping about the rocks as the Europeans stand on the shore waiting for their ships to take them back to their cities and the wedding between Miranda and Ferdinand.

That would be a happy end, a resolution as cozy as Job getting a new herd of sheep, camels, oxen, and she-asses. I've always thought that restitution to Job was somewhat ornamental and anticlimactic. Job's vindication and reward is that having declared who he is and what his claims are, the Lord answers him. This was the very thing that Job's comforters told him was impossible. The comforters say that Job must have broken one of the clauses of the covenant, that it should be just a clerical matter of rereading the rules. They say you can't address the Lord. But Job insists on himself, on his knowledge of himself. He declares who he is and who he conceives the Lord to be, not in detail but in mysterious living essence. The Lord appears and, having declared who he is—the creator of all things—says to Job's comforters, "Ye have not spoken of me the thing that is right as my servant Job hath."

If you think of justice as a set of rules, the way the comforters do, the book of Job is perplexingly unfair. The initial setup is that Satan gets to torture Job on a dare. Part of the reason for the perplexity is that the book of Job is an assemblage of different writings, by different authors, probably at different times. But the genius of it, in the parts sandwiched between the old-folktale beginning and the folktale ending, is Job's standing on his definition of himself. He is a creature of the Lord to be sure—"Hast thou not poured me out as milk, and curdled me like cheese?"—but a creature with an identity and a knowledge of that identity, who therefore can ask the identity of his antagonist. The answer is overwhelming. Whoever wrote the Lord's recitation of the order of things—the part where God speaks to Job out of the whirlwind—was as brilliant as the writer of Genesis, of which this nature poem is a recapitulation in equally magnificent but less benign terms. This revelation, this acknowledgment of identity, of Job's standing, and of Job's having said the right thing are the award and fulfillment of Job's trial.

Jung wrote an essay on Job, a blend of humanist psychology and belief. The main point of it is that Job's function as a creature of God is to remind God that he is not only all powerful but to recall him to his goodness.

The only villain in Job, by the way, is Satan. The three comforters (there is a fourth, but he comes in late and to my mind doesn't add a lot) are good. They are earnestly trying to help. This is what they do when they first come to him: "So they sat down with him upon the ground seven days and seven nights, and none spoke a word unto him: for they saw that his grief was very great."

Another notion that has been creeping up on me is that I have a fondness for stories in which the characters oppose each other not out of ill will but out of blind or partly occluded good intentions. To some extent, I'm qualifying Aristotle's remark that "among friends there is no justice." He's speaking of distributive justice, the pie sharing. A sweet example of blind good intentions is O. Henry's "The Gift of the Magi." A more elaborate case is Joyce Cary's trilogy *Herself Surprised*, *To Be a Pilgrim*, and *The Horse's Mouth*. Each volume is narrated by its protagonist, and while you are reading each one you are sympathetic to the wishes of each of the three characters. They cause each other a great deal of grief over the years through their pursuing the wishes that are consonant with their natures: but none is anything like a villain. The writer is just—in the simple sense of equal time, in the sense of symmetry (equal weight, equal sympathy on the part of the writer and reader), and in the most important sense of having the characters both oppose each other and sense each other as similar beings, maddening to each other because they must acknowledge each other and fulfilling to each other because each acknowledgment of another is an increase in one's own dimensions.

The examples of storytelling I've mentioned—from my sophomores' love stories up through O. Henry, Henry James, Joyce Cary, Shakespeare's *The Merchant of Venice* and *The Tempest*, and the book of Job—have always struck me as having something to do with my notion of justice. At first I did think it was as simple as an equal-time doctrine. Then I reverted to the stresses-and-strains theory: something like a Newton's third-law conception of conflict—"For every action there is an equal and opposite reaction"—and that it was the writer's job to create that symmetry. I'm not throwing these constructs aside as useless. But I have begun to think that a more crucial element of justice—the one most important to storytellers deploying their fictitious people— is found at that passage from lyric to dramatic; that first shiver of yourself in your own skin when you realize simultaneously that you can make claims and that there is someone else who can make claims on you. That acknowledgment of another being is a beginning, and when all is said and done, it is also the outcome—more than camels and she-asses, more than a fair share of the island—that we would value most: that our adversary see and acknowledge our likeness one to the other.

WHAT'S FUNNY

Note that there's no question mark. A bold omission.
Too bold? An essay means an attempt.

There's some pondering, some admiring, some
how-to. Also some funny quotations.

MY EARLIEST memory of what's funny is that it meant trouble. Someone had done or was doing something indecorous,
insubordinate, or inappropriate. Inappropriate. "Johnny,
that is inappropriate behavior! And don't you laugh either,
Tommy Flynn." Inappropriate. What a scolding, Pecksniffian,
thin-lipped, cold-blooded, brittle, airless, nasal Aunt-Polly-
taking-Tom-Sawyer-by-the-ear word. It is Malvolio telling the
roistering Sir Toby Belch that he should mend his ways. So I
cheer for Sir Toby's boozy answer: "Dost think because thou'rt
virtuous, there shall be no more cakes and ale?"

That was my first idea—that laughter is on the side of the bad boys—a small portion of relief for those under the thumbs of Sister Margaret Mary, drill sergeants, customs officials, maître d's at French restaurants. It is encouragement for sassy counterattack by those accused of being inappropriate.

A half-dozen ideas buzzed in. I looked for help from psychological and philosophical experts, ancient and modern. I discovered that the subject of humor has a vast bibliography, almost none of which is useful as how-to advice. I went to a lecture and heard some Freud. None of the jokes that Freud gives as examples of humor are at all funny. Someone said they were funnier in German and people laughed.

I was happier with a book called *Laughter* (*Le rire*) by Henri Bergson, and it's worthwhile, partly because once in a while his examples of humor are funny and partly because he directly contradicts my first notion that we laugh to cheer up the misfits. Bergson thinks that laughter is a way to bring the misfits in line. He believes in society in a wonderfully optimistic way; he believes that there is a shared social consciousness that punishes crime with legal penalties and lesser antisocial behavior with laughter. "Our laughter is always the laughter of a group . . . However spontaneous it seems, laughter always implies a kind of freemasonry or even complicity with other laughers, real or imaginary." And later he adds, "Laughter is a kind of social 'ragging,' a method of 'breaking in' people to the forms and conventions of society, a way of curbing eccentricity and unsociability in their early stages."

This idea is a more democratic version of a line of thought I'd heard at the lecture. For the ancients (Aristotle, Cicero, Quintillian, et al.), comedy was satire, a reproval of vices, and Renaissance followers of this line—for example, Thomas Hobbes and Baldassare Castiglione—thought laughter was chiefly used as a way of putting people in their place, of maintaining hierarchy against upstarts. Of the philosophers and social theorists mentioned, only Baruch Spinoza goes for joie de vivre as a cause of laughter. Later on he was joined by Henry Fielding, the only writer mentioned so far who actually made readers laugh.

To continue with Bergson. Laughter is not in sympathy with the aberrant person. "Try for a moment to become interested in everything that is being said and done; act in imagination with those who act, and feel with those who feel." No laughter. "Now step aside, look upon life as a disinterested spectator: many a drama will turn into comedy. It is enough for us to stop our ears to the sound of music in a room where dancing is going on for the dancers at once to appear ridiculous."

A shorter version of this lack-of-sympathy theory is a remark by Mel Brooks: "Comedy is when you get eaten by a lion. Tragedy is when I cut myself shaving."

This notion is borne out by the experience of an actor friend of mine. He had to take a pratfall on stage. When he fell far upstage, everyone laughed. When he fell halfway downstage, everyone laughed except the first two rows. When he fell right on the lip of the stage, nobody laughed. Several people in the front row, who'd heard the thump of his hipbone, said, "Ow!" This actor's experience may put to rest the facile theory of humor as malice, that we laugh at someone slipping on a banana peel because we're mean. We're not mean—we say "ow," at least if we're close. As we get farther away we become cartoon watchers.

It turned out that what Bergson thinks laughter is reproving isn't roister-doister, isn't social misfits because they're misfits per se—what laughter is reproving is *inelasticity*. One way he begins to make this clear is by pointing out that most tragedies are named for the principal character. *Andromaque, Phèdre, Le Cid.* It's true for William Shakespeare as well as for Jean Racine and Pierre Corneille. *Hamlet, Macbeth, Othello.* Molière's comedies are called *The Would-be Gentleman* (*Le bourgeois gentil-homme*), *The Miser* (*L'Avare*), *The Pretentious Ladies* (*Les précieuses ridicules*), *The Imaginary Invalid* (*Le malade imaginaire*). They are named for a vice or a pretension. In the tragedies the main character has more than one quality, is pulled back and forth between qualities. In comedies the main character is a marionette, and all the strings attach to one quality, often one that the character is blind to. The tragic characters are more or less aware of their qualities, but in any case they are trying to adapt. The comic characters are not; they are operating in mechanical obedience to their obsessive quality. They are inorganic, and Bergson's idea of good social life is that it is organic, always in a process of vital adjustment.

A variation on a character who is comic because controlled mechanically by one quality is a character who believes that things are happening mechanically when they are not. Bergson cites a passage in *Tartarin sur les Alpes* in which "Bompard makes Tartarin . . . accept the idea of Switzerland chock-full of machinery, like the basement of the Opera House, and run by a company which maintains a series of waterfalls, glaciers and artificial crevasses." (This may have been a funnier idea before the late twentieth-century invention of theme parks—now it might just be scary.)

A friend of mine owns a hundred-ton Newfoundland schooner. One summer Martin Scorsese was making a movie of the novel *The Age of Innocence*. There's a scene in which the hero is looking at the heroine who is standing by the sea. He says to himself something like this: "If that schooner passes the lighthouse before she turns around, it's all over." Winona Ryder was hired to play the part of the heroine; my friend's schooner was hired to play the part of the schooner. An assistant director was buzzing back and forth in a speedboat, talking to Mr. Scorsese by walkie-talkie and to the schooner by bullhorn. He yelled through his bullhorn, "Action," and the crew weighed anchor and hoisted the sails. The assistant director yelled, "Go past the lighthouse!" The sails filled, the bow wave began to gurgle. A minute later, the assistant director listened intently to his walkie-talkie and then yelled through his bullhorn, "Hold it right there! . . . Now back it up a few feet!" and then added as an afterthought, "Winona sneezed."

The repeated Bergsonian formula for the comic is "the mechanical encrusted on the living" and the living schooner and the mechanically minded assistant director fit neatly.

So far so good. But there are a few quibbles. According to Bergson, repetition or duplication inevitably suggest the mechanical. If we see two people onstage doing exactly the same thing we laugh. The more the merrier. Yes—sometimes. But are the Rockettes funny? It's not entirely a rhetorical question. By themselves they're impressive and kind of sexy. What might make the mechanical aspect more apparent and therefore comic is the kind of thing we've seen in a score of movies: the heroine or hero gets mixed up in the Rockettes or their equivalent—she faces the wrong way, her face is in anxious movement, in contrast to the fixed smiles of the Rockettes, perhaps she almost gets kicked. She's like Charlie Chaplin, caught in the huge cogs of the machinery in *Modern Times*. But that we have to make an adjustment points to a crack in the veneer of the shiny theory.

A stronger quibble is with the idea that the mechanization of the human body is funny per se. Frankenstein's monster isn't funny. We could make him funny: Abbot and Costello meet Frankenstein . . .

Before picking on Bergson some more, I'd like to say that his book does belong on the short shelf of works helpful to writers—alongside Konstantin Stanislavski's *An Actor Prepares*, Aristotle's *Poetics* and Vladimir Nabokov's *Speak, Memory*. Of these, only the

Nabokov is a work of art. The others are uphill going, but the view is worth the climb.

As ingenious and sometimes fruitful as the encrustation-of-the-mechanical-on-the-living theory is, there are other ways to explain the same funny event. The passage from Bergson that put me in mind of the schooner story is this: "[W]hen reading the newspaper I came across a specimen of the comic . . . a large steamer was wrecked off the coast of Dieppe. With considerable difficulty some of the passengers were rescued in a boat. A few customs-house officers, who had courageously rushed to their assistance, began by asking them 'if they had anything to declare.'"

Bergson isn't very good at telling a funny story. There are two weak points. One is the phrase "some of the passengers were rescued in a boat." This implied to me, for a moment at least, that other passengers drowned, and I became sympathetically alarmed. More awkwardnesses arise in the next overelaborate compound sentence. "A few of the customs-house officers, who had courageously rushed to their assistance . . ." Their rushing to the rescue is a piece of action better put in its proper chronological order and in its own sentence—after the wreck but before they all gather on shore. It is also odd that "a few customs-house officers . . . began by asking them . . ." were the officers speaking in chorus. Clarity, clarity, clarity. And then the punch line loses immediacy by being cast in indirect speech rather than direct—"Have you anything to declare?"

I'd also like to see the passengers, just a glimpse. Probably missing various articles of clothing, wouldn't you think? Water pouring out of the pockets of the men's frock coats. The women's ringlets clinging to their cheeks like strands of a wet mop.

A good exercise for someone interested in comic scenes would be to rewrite the incident. Where to start? What point of view? How to have the shipwreck frightening but not mortal? Everything true enough, so that the customs officer's question is wildly incongruous.

Incongruous. Out of proportion. Is it just the officer's mechanical response that is comic? I think we also need the largeness of the large steamer, and although Bergson doesn't bring it up, it might help if there were some enormous waves rolling in from a North Atlantic storm. If this whole affair were about a rowboat that overturned while crossing the Rhine on its way to a customs house in Strasbourg, there might still be some contrast between an emergency and being asked a silly question but not the contrast between the force of the sea, which has just tossed around a ship the size of a shopping mall, and the suddenly pipsqueak voice of human regulation.

Incongruity comes in different modes. One thing doesn't fit with another because it is too big or too small. A small child wearing her father's overcoat. A three-hundred-pound man wearing a thong bikini. Or they're the wrong shape: a square peg in a round hole, or a long sofa being carried up a two-turn stairway. Or of incompatible textures—something that's flaccid when it should be stiff: trying to use a wet noodle as a pipe cleaner, is what came to my mind.

Incongruity, like the encrusted mechanical, isn't necessarily funny, but it is often an auxiliary or a catalyst to a comic scene.

Topsy-Turvy

Reversal of fortune is Aristotle's favorite tragic plot. But in tragedy it comes after a long struggle, and we are as sympathetically aware of the inner turmoil of the main character as we are of the objective events. The doom is an inevitable consequence of the relation between the internal and the external. Topsy-turvy also is a reversal, but with an oops-a-daisy swoop of suddenness. The primal form of topsy-turvy is jouncing a baby on your knee. "This is the way the ladies ride—trot, trot," and then the gentlemen canter, the huntsmen gallop, until "Here comes the country boy" and you swoop the kid into space from one side to the other saying, "Hobbledehoy! Hobbledehoy!" Or the New England variant: "Trot trot to Boston, trot trot to Lynn. Look out, Maud, you're going to . . . *fall* in!"

If it gets a laugh, it's because of the gasp of weightlessness, and then it's all right again. But there has been, in the midst of the usual gravity, a sudden alternative.

Oscar Wilde's wit thrives on the sudden unexpected alternative. When he was on tour in America, he was taken to Niagara Falls. His escort said, "Will you look at that. Isn't it amazing?"

Wilde said, "It would be amazing . . . if it went up."

The reason Wilde was on tour, by the way, is that Gilbert & Sullivan had had a great success in England with their show *Patience, or Bunthorne's Bride.* The main character of fun is a poet who swans around in a lovely velvet jacket with a lily in his hand. Gilbert and Sullivan wanted to put the show on in America, but they were afraid Americans wouldn't get the joke, so they secretly funded Wilde's tour and sent their play along in his footsteps.

Back to Niagara Falls. "Oh come now, Mr. Wilde," one of the white-gloved matrons said. "It is such an inspiring sight that couples come here on their honeymoon."

Wilde said, "Then it must be the second biggest disappointment in a young bride's life."

In *The Importance of Being Earnest* a lot of the comedy is topsy-turvy, particularly in its turning the English caste system on its ear.

> ACT ONE, SCENE ONE.
>
> Morning-room in ALGERNON's flat . . . The room is luxuriously and artistically furnished. The sound of a piano is heard in the adjoining room. LANE [the butler] is arranging afternoon tea on the table, and after the music has ceased, ALGERNON enters.

> ALGERNON: Did you hear what I was playing, Lane?
> LANE: I didn't think it polite to listen, sir.

After some to-and-fro about the servants drinking the champagne and Algernon asking Lane about Lane's married state, Algernon abruptly but languidly says, "I don't know that I am much interested in your family life, Lane."

> LANE: No, sir; it is not a very interesting subject. I never think of it myself.

A bit later, Algernon, in an aside: "Lane's views on marriage seem somewhat lax. Really, if the lower orders don't set us a good example, what on earth is the use of them?"

Each one of the men, while remaining in their apparently undisruptable master-servant relation, catches the other off-balance and executes a verbal judo throw. Algernon's enthusiasm for his own piano playing is met not with direct contradiction but with a sidestep and a foot sweep of wicked politeness. Algernon's dismissal of Lane's family life is met with such total agreement that it is as if Lane fell on his back and flipped Algernon up and over.

But Algernon lands on his feet and, with a comic turn of his own, twists the conventional wisdom, about the correspondence of the social and moral order, upside down.

And now he's ready for Jack, Lady Bracknell, Gwendolen, Cecily, Miss Prism, and the Reverend Doctor Chasuble.

Cecily and Gwendolen also flip each other, but sometimes each achieves a sudden weightlessness on her own. In the following passage Gwendolen and Cecily are quarreling with exquisite correctness. The Ernest in question is, of course, both Algernon and Jack.

> GWENDOLEN [QUITE POLITELY, RISING]: My darling Cecily, I think there must be some slight error. Mr. Ernest Worthington is engaged to me. The announcement will appear in the Morning Post on Saturday at the latest.
> CECILY [VERY POLITELY, RISING]: I am afraid you must be under some misconception. Ernest proposed to me exactly ten minutes ago. [Shows diary].
> GWENDOLEN [EXAMINES DIARY THROUGH HER LOR-GNETTE CAREFULLY]: It is very curious, for he asked me to be his wife yesterday afternoon at 5:30. If you would care to verify the incident, pray do so. [Produces diary of her own.] I never travel without my diary. One should always have something sensational to read in the train.

Riffs go on.

> CECILY [THOUGHTFULLY AND SADLY]: Whatever unfortunate entanglement my dear boy may have got into, I will never reproach him with it after we are married.

GWENDOLEN: Do you allude to me, Miss Cardew, as an entanglement? You are presumptuous. On an occasion of this kind it becomes more than a moral duty to speak one's mind. It becomes a pleasure.

Neither Mr. Wilde nor we are laughing at the innocently intent maidens in order to reprove their faults. On the contrary, we are happy to see them wafting lightly upward into the realm where pleasure is more than moral duty and narcissism is just one of many sweet odors to be savored.

There is an additional comic skill at work here, perhaps not readily apparent in extracted passages. The broad comedy of masquerade and deception—Algernon and Jack both pretending to be Ernest, the mystery of Jack's parentage, Lady Bracknell's snobbism capsized—is an old but worthy tune played on the A string of Wilde's violin. What produces the sense of life being lighter than air is that Wilde is simultaneously trilling on the E string, double-bowing hemi-demi-semi-quavers. The trills wouldn't be as good without the tune.

Wilde's lighthearted nimble bad-boy reflexes unfortunately did him in. When he sued the Marquis of Queensbury for libel— the Marquis had referred to Wilde as a sodomite—Sir Edward Carson was the lawyer for the defense. When Wilde was in the witness box, Carson hammered away at him about his having entertained a stable boy: Did you invite him to dinner? Did you give him wine? Did you . . . did you . . . did you?

"Did you ever kiss him?"

Wilde said, "Oh dear no."

Carson paused. This pause has become famous among trial lawyers. The Carson pause.

Wilde said, "He was a peculiarly plain boy. He was, unfortunately, extremely ugly."

SIR EDWARD CARSON went on to become an Ulster Unionist leader. Oscar Fingal O'Flahertie Wills Wilde lost his civil case, was then prosecuted criminally, and went to jail. He wrote *De profundis* there, "The Ballad of Reading Gaol" shortly thereafter, and died in exile three years later. I don't know but hope that it is true that Wilde's last words in a run-down hotel room in France were these: "Either that wallpaper goes, or I do."

TO RETURN TO our own land and the subject of the comic as a function of abrupt inversion—there is this report from volume II of Shelby Foote's history of the Civil War: General Bragg, having been driven east through most of Tennessee and on past Chattanooga, won the battle of Chickamauga for the South. Longstreet and Polk urged him to follow through and destroy Rosencran's Northern army completely. Bragg wasn't sure the Northerners were in such utter retreat, in spite of the loud cheers of his own troops.

> [A] Confederate private who had been captured the previous day, escaped and made his way back to his outfit. When he told his captain what he had seen across the way—for instance that the Unionists were abandoning their wounded as they slogged northward . . . he was taken at once to repeat his story, first to his regimental and brigade commanders, then to Bragg himself. The stern-faced general heard him out, but was doubtful, if not of the soldier's capacity for accurate description, then at any rate of his judgment on such a

complicated matter. 'Do you know what a retreat looks like?' he asked.

'I ought to, General,' he said. 'I've been with you during your whole campaign.'"

Who laughed then?

To laugh at a private getting the better of a general, you have to be a civilian or have the soul of a civilian under your gold braid. Do you also have to be at least momentarily unaware of what was outside and less than a mile from Bragg's tent, which was ten thousands dead? Shelby Foote writes, "[T]he butcher's bill [of dead and wounded] North and South, came to 16,170 and 18,454 respectively. The combined total of 34,624 was exceeded only the three-day slaughter at Gettysburg."

In Bragg's tent, who laughed?

We can't know. Shelby Foote doesn't tell us. Can you imagine who might have laughed then? An attendant brigadier, colonel, major, or captain? And if he'd come to the tent through the field of dead, what would you think of his laughter? Would you think it inappropriate? Or would you see it as relief, a short, earned leave from service at the front? I can imagine laughter as a reaction to horror or grief but how much better if there is something comic to accommodate it.

Shelby Foote does tell us this: "[What the private said] endeared him to his comrades, then and thereafter, when it was repeated, as it often was, around campfires and at future veteran gatherings." I laughed when I read what the private said. In Shelby Foote's book it comes before the listing of the dead and wounded. It is on a printed page, here and now, not then and there.

Another sudden inversion. Giorgio Bassani's novel, *The Garden of the Finzi-Continis* is about a Jewish family in Italy during

the 1930s and World War II. The Italian Fascists didn't system-
atically kill Jews, but they treated them in a way that made it
possible for the Nazis to ship them to concentration camps after
the collapse of the Italian government. However, the prologue
to the novel includes a scene that takes place after the war. A
family and friends drive to Cerveteri to have a picnic among
the Etruscan tombs, a usual and popular Roman outing. On the
ride back to Rome the narrator is enjoying the view of the sea
through the pine trees. They're all happy—except the little girl.
The girl's father asks her what's wrong.

> "It was sad."
> "What was sad?"
> "The Etruscans."
> "But, Gianina, they died, oh, three thousand years ago."
> Gianina says, "What difference does that make?"[1]

A SUDDEN ALTERNATIVE, an upending of complacency. It's certainly not comic. Does the topsy-turvy theory therefore fail? I
think not, but it needs help. Perhaps none of the factors—neither
distance, nor encrustation of the mechanical, nor incongruity,
nor topsy-turvy—works in isolation. And, more important, if
one of the factors is at odds with the others, the comic effect
becomes something else. What the girl said put us at a distance
from the picnic party, but it also removed the distance of three

---

1. My version of the conversation between father and daughter is a syn-
opsis from memory of a longer passage. For that, see either *Il giardino dei
Finzi-Contini*, Enaudi, Milan, 1962 or *The Garden of the Finzi-Contini*, Athe-
neum, 1965. It is a beautiful, sad novel. Sometimes one remembers a passage not entirely accurately but in a version that is a distilled residue of
what was so moving thirty-three years ago.

thousand years. Either by reason of ignorance or innocence or simply standing outside of time, she didn't think of the Etruscans as far away. More important, for the narrator riding beside her in the open car under the pines, what she said also removed whatever distance he had managed to put between himself and the deportation of the Finzi-Continis, between himself and their unfindable graves.

PRECISION & IMMEDIACY

We noticed that Bergson, in retelling the story of the large steamer and the customs officer, made his point, but he also made the telling somewhat awkward and as flightless as a dodo. There was a need for order, precision, and direct, immediate speech. I also suggested more details, and that suggestion may be a problem. Details can either make a story more immediately visible or slow the pace. A lot of the art of storytelling, not just funny storytelling, is in the balance between detail and pace. Both are necessary to immediacy—it's sort of like being able to believe in the particle theory of light and the wave theory simultaneously.

If you are putting a comedy on stage, the two oldest rules in the book are pace and bright light. You don't want shadows or sight lines into darkness. But what is this bright light to someone putting prose on a page? I think the translation is precision.

A by-the-way piece of circumstantial evidence: any fiction writer who gives a public reading is often surprised when the audience laughs at a passage the writer thought was just simple clear description. But, coupled with the goodwill of the audience and the slight nervous tension in the room, simple clear description has the effect of sudden illumination. And bright light or its equivalent has another happy effect: you realize that you are going to be shown things so clearly that you aren't going to have to think.

Precision is a component of wit, which is sometimes comic and sometimes just a bit different. It must be precise, perhaps even more precise, but sometimes it makes you think and that detour between words and the blossoming of them in the inner senses, that detour by way of thinking, produces a pleasure that is too slow to trigger the physical response of laughter.

The Duke of La Rochefoucauld wrote relatively few pages, but he worked his maxims over and over. It is true that he spent a great deal of time making love and war, but once he settled down he wrote and rewrote, polishing his brief remarks until they became, at their best, as spare as haiku: "We all have enough strength to endure the misfortunes of others."

La Rochefoucauld was careful not to use either obsolete or out-of-the-way words, or words that he thought were not likely to survive. There are no references to the military equipment of the seventeenth century, nor to customs, dress, or architecture. In his ambition to leave a text that would not require footnotes, he has been successful. This is an exercise that the French have greatly admired, and also two professors at Duke University who have written a style manual called *Clear and Simple as the Truth*, an awkward but finally justified title. La Rochefoucauld is their chief icon of classic style, and their initial quotation of his work is a description of a lady.

> *Mme de Chevreuse avait beaucoup d'esprit, d'ambition et de beauté; elle était galante, vive, hardie, entreprenante; elle se servait de tous ses charmes pour réussir dans ses desseins, et elle a presque toujours porté malheur aux personnes qu'elle y a engagées.*

Consider two possible translations.

translation 1

Madame de Chevreuse had sparkling intelligence, ambition, and beauty in plenty. She was flirtatious, lively, bold,
enterprising; she used all her charms to push her projects to
success, and she almost always brought disaster to those she
encountered on her way.

translation 2

Madame de Chevreuse had wit, ambition, and beauty;
she was flirtatious, lively, sure of herself and enterprising; she
used all her charms to further her plans, and to anyone she
involved in them, she almost always brought disaster. (Author's
translation.)

Neither translation really sews it up. The problem is partly the
particle *y*, which serves many purposes in French: it can mean
"there," "thereto or thereby," or "in," "for," "to or about," "me,"
"you," "he," "she," "it," "us," "them." But it can be inserted
neatly, like the tip of a finger on the first half-hitch of a knot
so that the final bit of tying will end up taut. The two translations handle the *y* problem differently, but the more important
difference is that the older translation (no. 1) is lengthened with
modifiers—"sparkling intelligence," "in plenty"—and the final
phrase "to those she encountered on her way" is a modifying
subordinate clause that dribbles off the end.

To modify, to improve exactness, or to leave spare? One
answer to that question is this parenthetical remark from an
Adam Mars-Jones story in which a man has just been convicted
of murder at the Old Bailey. The judge comes in with the bit of

black cloth on his head, which means bad news. The omniscient narrator comments, "The phrase 'I sentence you to death,' like the phrase 'I love you,' is better left unadorned."

That quoted passage could serve as an Occam's razor for anyone trying to write clearly and simply.

The polar opposite of the spare and ageless precision of the La Rochefoucauld is precision through abundance. Here is one footnote from David Foster Wallace's narrative of his Caribbean cruise on a luxury liner. The title is "A Supposedly Fun Thing I'll Never Do Again."

[40] This is related to the phenomenon of the Professional Smile, a national pandemic in the service industry; and noplace, in my experience have I been on the receiving end of as many Professional Smiles as I am on the *Nadir*: maitre d's, Chief Stewards, Hotel Managers' minions, Cruise Director—their P.S.'s all come on like switches at my approach. But also back on land at banks, restaurants, airline ticket counters, on and on. You know this smile—the strenuous contraction of circumoral fascia w/ incomplete zygomatic involvement—the smile that doesn't quite reach the smiler's eyes and that signifies nothing more than a calculated attempt to advance the smiler's own interests by pretending to like the smilee. Am I the only person who's sure that the growing number of cases in which totally average-looking people suddenly open up with automatic weapons in shopping malls and insurance offices and medical complexes and McDonald'ses is somehow causally related to the fact that these venues are well-known dissemination-loci of the Professional Smile?

And yet the Professional Smile's absence now *also* causes despair. Anybody who's ever bought a pack of gum in a Man-

hattan cigar store or asked for something to be stamped FRAG-
ILE at a Chicago post office, or tried to obtain a glass of water
from a South Boston waitress knows well the soul-crushing
effect of a service worker's scowl, i.e. the humiliation and
resentment of being denied the Professional Smile. And the
Professional Smile has by now skewed even my resentment at
the dreaded Professional Scowl: I walk away from the Man-
hattan tobacconist resenting not the counterman's character
or absence of goodwill but his lack of *professionalism* in denying
me the Smile. What a fucking mess.

This passage is a cascade, a torrential rant. But within the wave
the particles are particular. There is, for example, the highfa-
lutin anatomical terminology: the "circumoral fascia" and the
"incomplete zygomatic involvement." (I finally looked it up in the
online Free Dictionary—"pertaining to the zygoma." Okay. At
least it's on the same page. "Zygoma: the slender arch formed by
the temporal process of the cheekbone that bridges to the zygomatic process of the temporal bone.") This is mildly funny—the
guy is in such high dudgeon about these smiles that he obsesses
to the point of excessive but accurate research. He immediately
zags back from his zig into second-year med school lingo and
puts it in plain language: "the smile that doesn't quite reach the
smiler's eyes."

The next time he reverses field it's from the smile to the scowl,
that is, the denial of smile. And now he's moving faster—Man-
hattan, Chicago, South Boston—all quick cuts but with immediately recognizable detail fragments. By the end he's moving so
fast, and with such accumulated weight and friction, that he just
melts. "What a fucking mess."

So there's another, and last factor in this catalog of comic
effects: the melting or collapsing of an elaboration. I think the

rule is that the labor in the elaboration has to be honest labor. The writer has to take part as wholeheartedly in the construction as in the collapse. David Foster Wallace is serious about the Professional Smile; he builds a case that is eerily logical and rhetorically well made. At the same time he shoots himself off like a rocket with a loose fin.

A subcorollary to the honest-labor-in-elaboration theorem. I have heard from others and noticed in my own work that when a writer wants to let a character have a ridiculous, preposterously bad idea, if the idea is concocted, made out of a kit for bad ideas, there is little comic effect. If, on the other hand, the idea is a notion that I have once believed and held dear and only finally got over, then that idea planted in a character is more likely to have enough life to it to be truly funny.

Somewhere in the midst of Edward Gibbon's *Decline and Fall of the Roman Empire*, Gibbon quotes a French historian who says, "Nothing is beautiful if it's not true." That applies to what's funny too.

ARISTOTLE

Reading and applying the prime mover of liter-
ary criticism. He's more of a regular guy than I
thought—and he truly wants to help.

EDWARD GIBBON, the author of *The History of the Decline and Fall of the Roman Empire*, was beginning to be grouchy by the time he got to volume 7. It had been a long haul, and he still had two volumes to go. He had had some good reviews, and the eighteenth-century English literary set being like most literary sets but more so, he'd taken some licks.

But Gibbon made enough of a name for himself that he was presented at court. He made his several bows. King George looked at him blankly for a while, and then said, "Ah. Mr. Gibbon. Scribble, scribble, scribble."

So there may have been some bile mixed with his ink when, near the beginning of Volume 7, he got to describing the state of the Byzantine army. He dutifully read through their many manuals and treatises on tactics and strategy. His summary of the Byzantine state of preparedness was brief: "The discipline of a soldier is formed by exercise rather than by study; the battles won by lessons of tactics may be numbered with the epic poems created from the rules of criticism."

Whatever double-edged spleen there may be in that sentence, it is a good thing to remember in the back-and-forth about theory and practice. I once was at a dinner table with a bunch of classical scholars who were discussing commentaries on *The Odyssey*. They seemed puzzled by some basic facts about rowing and sailing. I'm afraid I said, "Maybe you guys should spend some time in boats." Gibbon was more elegant.

So why on earth am I going to have a go at Aristotle's *Poetics*? It is a difficult and uncertain text but one that has enthralled and puzzled scholars, dramatists, and story writers of all kinds.

It has given rise to some brittle rule making, but I think that what Aristotle actually said is more by way of suggested principles, carefully proceeding from basic notions:

"Tragedy is an imitation of an action that is complete, and whole, and of a certain magnitude. . . . A whole is that which has a beginning, a middle, and an end. A beginning is that which does not follow by causal necessity, but after which something naturally is or comes to be. An end . . . is that which itself naturally follows some other thing . . . but has nothing following it. A middle is that which follows something as some other thing follows it."

This is as hard to read as an insurance contract, but Aristotle is getting his ducks in a row so he can get on with his bigger and better ideas. For my own purposes I gathered bits and pieces from other translations. I now have this version by heart: The beginning has nothing necessarily before it. The middle has something necessarily before and something necessarily after it. The end has something necessarily before it and nothing necessarily after it. This isn't as hard to read, but some people may say, "Well, duh." I like it because it sticks in my mind like a skip rope chant.

One reason there are variations in translations of the *Poetics* is that the text that has come down to us is fragmentary and spotty. It is unclear what the text *is*. It may have been the notes one of Aristotle's students took. It may have been some pages of a textbook, possibly by Aristotle, possibly by a disciple.

The *Poetics* had two parts—one about tragedy, the other about comedy. The part about comedy has never been found.

Aristotle was interested in everything. He wrote or lectured on natural history, politics, ethics, medicine. I think that part of his reason for talking about tragedy was to bring an orderly understanding of epics and drama to his fellow citizens. That is why he begins by stating what seems obvious.

I think that another part of his urge was that he was a fan. I imagine his unstated purpose was something like this: "You epic story tellers and dramatists have given me a great deal of pleasure. You have often taken my breath away. I'd like to point out the ways you've done this, to *analyze* my pleasure. I'd also like to offer some opinions on how you can give me even more pleasure."

That is an admirable stance for a critic.

What else does wholeness require besides beginning, middle, and end? He goes on to say, ". . . the imitation is one when the object imitated is one, so the plot . . . must imitate one action and that a whole, the structural union of the parts being such that, if any one of them is displaced or removed, the whole will be disjointed and disturbed."

So—unity of action or actions linked by necessity, that is, by causality. Although Aristotle is dealing with human action and motivation, these are echoes of his observations of nature, of how plants and animals are begotten and grow. We'll get to how he accounts for free will later on.

"Unity of plot does not, as some persons think, consist in the unity of the hero. For infinitely various are the incidents in one man's life which cannot be reduced to unity . . ."

For a moment I thought he was going to go for more than one protagonist, as in *War and Peace*, which has two main leads, Andrei and Pierre. It turns out he's saying that one man is a necessary but not sufficient condition.

On the subject of unity Aristotle says, "Tragedy endeavors, as far as possible, to confine itself to a single revolution of the sun or but slightly to exceed this limit." I think it was the French neoclassicists who made the unities iron clad. One action, one man, one day. Aristotle allows for some flexibility.

But still—why this yearning for unity? This insistence that all the parts of the story cohere? Is it just Aristotle's liking order?

There is a basis for thinking that we humans crave order. There have even been experiments with chimpanzees, our fellow primates. They were given paint and canvas and encouraged to make art. It turned out that some of the chimpanzees got good at it. On their own they made pictures that filled the canvas with symmetrical designs that look like sunsets or fanlike plants. One of the chimpanzees, Congo, made a number of sales. Picasso bought several Congo paintings. I got this news from a book called *The Biology of Art* by Desmond Morris, a former curator of the London Zoo. There were further experiments. A chimpanzee was given a canvas with a blank square already painted on it, each side of the square several inches in from the edge of the canvas. The chimpanzee did his painting completely within the blank square. The next step was to give the chimpanzee a canvas with a small square in the middle of it. The chimpanzee was momentarily puzzled but, after a bit of thought, painted a picture around the square, incorporating it into his design.

Kurt Vonnegut took on this question of design order in a by-the-way remark. One day in the middle of a workshop he said, more or less, "Why are we doing this? Why are we making up stories? I think I know why painters do it. Painters look at the mess of life and decide that at least in their pictures they're going to make something that makes sense. The picture may be of something horrible, but it'll be clear. I think we ought to be in the same business."

So Aristotle, Congo, and Vonnegut are in convergence on the question of order. Aristotle however wants more than formal order: "[a]n imitation of an action that is complete and whole *and of a certain magnitude*" (italics added). On the question of magnitude, he says, after going on a bit about the beauty of living creatures, "In a creature of vast size, or say 1,000 miles long . . . instead of the object being seen all at once, the unity and wholeness are lost to the beholder. . . . So a story or plot must be of some length, but of a length to be taken in by the memory." So there's an outer limit, but he still wants something big. "The longer the story, consistently with its being comprehensible as a whole, the finer it is by reason of its magnitude. As a rough general formula a length which allows of the hero passing by a series of probable and necessary stages from bad fortune to good or from good to bad, may suffice as a limit for the magnitude."

But why? Why is it better to have the form filled to the brim with content?

"Tragedy is an imitation *not only* of a complete action but also of incidents arousing pity and fear" (italics added). Pity *and* fear.

Aristotle has reservations about a plot that has a good man

passing from good fortune to bad. We feel only pity at completely undeserved misfortune.

Aristotle is no happier about a bad man passing from good fortune to bad—that's just how it should be. A bad man passing from bad fortune to good is simply odious.

"There remains then the intermediate kind of personage, a man not *preeminently* virtuous and just, whose misfortune . . . is brought upon him not by vice or depravity but by some fault."

I guess someone preeminently virtuous and just wouldn't get into trouble—unless by bad luck. And then our reaction is "What a pity." But the "intermediate personage" is someone like most of us and so we feel a sympathetic fear. Is that it? But Aristotle also says, "In tragedy the characters are better than we are; in comedy they are worse." That is a harder notion. I took up the question of comedy in another chapter called "What's Funny." A comic character has a foible, not a horrible vice but something that controls him, and he dances to it like a puppet on a string. So a comic character is worse because at the mercy of his foible.

But how is a tragic character better than we are?

There are parts of the *Poetics* that seem to say that "better" means someone of a great family. However there are scholars who think that Aristotle brings up great families because they provide good material. The House of Atreus comes to mind—a father kills his daughter, his wife kills him, the son kills her. There are causes for all three, ostensibly good causes, and all have terrible consequences.

One thing that makes the tragic characters "better" than the comic characters is that they do what they do on purpose. They have the will and the energy to try to set things right. The consequences go wrong.

I can understand that "better" as a more drastic and violent form of advice I got from a very smart friend. He told me that he didn't like my stories that had dumb and/or bad characters. He said, "I like the stories where everyone is trying to do the right thing and it still ends up in a mess."

But what is harder to figure out is why Aristotle loves the play *Oedipus the King*. How does that square with "better" and "fault" and "misfortune"? Isn't Oedipus just doomed?

And what *is* the misfortune of Oedipus? Is it the fact that he killed his father and married his mother? He didn't know that the man he quarreled with at the crossroads was his father, nor that the man was the king of Thebes.

Oedipus then saves Thebes from a plague and is greeted as a hero. He marries the widowed queen. He doesn't have any idea . . .

Is this misfortune? Or is the misfortune that he finds out? Is he an "intermediate personage not preeminently virtuous or just whose misfortune . . . is brought upon him not by vice or depravity but by some fault"?

Jean Cocteau wrote the book for the opera of *Oedipus the King*. Cocteau's reading is that the gods laid a snare for Oedipus. That's too neat. And it reduces Oedipus to a completely helpless victim. There *was* a prophecy that Oedipus would kill his father and marry his mother. And that is his fate. But it is not just a case of "you can run but you can't hide." There is a moment when Oedipus's faults bring upon him the misfortune of knowing *and* bring the truth out publicly so that Oedipus also brings Jocasta to her doom. If Oedipus had listened to the blind man or to Jocasta, he could have vanished, borne all the burden alone.

We all have dooms—we now call them, among other things, genes. But we have choice at the margins. When Oedipus learned about this prophecy, he fled from Corinth because he thought that the king and queen of Corinth were his real parents. This is a good course of action. It is while wandering in his self-imposed exile that he kills the king of Thebes, not knowing who the man is.

When Oedipus is asked by a priest of Thebes to save the city once again, by solving the murder that has brought a pestilence, Oedipus says yes, he is the king, it's his job. So far so good. But being king has had an effect on him. When his brother-in-law Creon brings the news from the Delphic oracle that the reason Thebes is suffering yet again is that there is an unavenged killing, Oedipus vows to find the killer. But when Creon brings in a blind seer, Oedipus begins to behave badly. He thinks Creon is out to get the throne. Power can beget two things in an odd simultaneity: arrogance *and* paranoia.

Oedipus pursues his own investigation energetically and ruthlessly. He has a witness roughed up to force him to speak. The truth comes out bit by bit; Oedipus is the killer of the old king. Oedipus is shaken by this, but at least he isn't guilty of patricide and incest.

More news: the king of Corinth has died of old age. Oedipus grieves but also feels relief. But there's yet more news—the king and queen of Corinth weren't his real parents. A shepherd found the infant Oedipus who'd been left to die on a hillside. That shepherd passed him to another shepherd who passed him on to the king and queen of Corinth.

Oedipus's wife, Jocasta, tries to stop him at this point. He suspects that she wants him to stop because she doesn't want it to come out that she married a waif, a shepherd's boy. He even exalts that he, a foundling, rose to become a king.

Jocasta says, "You are fatally wrong! May you never learn who you are!"

Oedipus says, "Go, one of you, and bring the shepherd here. Let us leave this woman to brag of her royal name."

Does Jocasta think that the misfortune is finding out the

truth? If the answer is yes, then Oedipus's *fault* is his arrogance and ruthless investigation. However abhorrent patricide and incest are, he didn't commit them out of vice or depravity.

Does that answer stand? It has a logic, but perhaps a lawyer's logic. It leaves out the terrible undoing of a man. It's not just that Oedipus can't go on being king. He is filled with self-revulsion. All the love he felt for Jocasta—and he did truly love her—is infected. His love for his two daughters is infected.

When the truth comes out in public, Jocasta goes into the palace and hangs herself. Oedipus finds her body. He takes out two of her golden hairpins and pierces his eyes.

I think that piercing, in a terrible and terrifying way, is a sign of his love for her. The hairpins are the nearest things at hand, but I can't help thinking that taking out her hairpins was something he'd done many, many times as the two of them prepared to go to bed.

It is also an extension—a magnification—of an ordinary human reaction to a horrible sight: we close our eyes, we cover our eyes with our hands. Oedipus is moved to do more than shield his eyes. Perhaps he hopes to blot out forever what he sees. There is pity, there is compassion. It is human to wish not to see; it is human to block grief by hurting ourselves. There is also terror in the contemplation of what Oedipus will go on seeing in his endless blind sight.

I think Aristotle means by magnitude not just a full chain of incidents, not just an undoing of a man of high estate, but this *magnification* of grief and horror.

Last Night in Twisted River, a recent novel by John Irving, has a writer as the hero. The writer gets lots of good advice. Some of it is advice that Irving himself actually got. There is one bit that

I'm guessing Irving made up. An older writer tells the hero that the hero is "dodging the squeamish stuff," that a writer shouldn't back off from what makes him feel squeamish—or makes the reader feel squeamish. By itself that could be dangerous advice. The caution, which Irving knows full well, is that there be causality, that the story lead inevitably to the horrifying act. Don't turn back from what your story has led you to.

Wholeness isn't just a matter of setting up a form and filling it. It isn't just coloring inside the lines.

One time I was trying to discuss the *Poetics* with a teacher at Saint John's, the Great Books college. He said, "Have you read the *Physics*?" I said I'd tried but found it puzzling. The Great Books guy said, "You can't understand the *Poetics* unless you understand the *Physics*." The *Physics* by the way isn't the science of Newton or Einstein; it's what used to be called natural history. It's a contemplation of how things grow, of how plants and animals become what they are actually meant to be, of how things fulfill their natural form.

The Great Books guy was being snotty, possibly because I'd said that another of my reactions to the *Physics*, aside from puzzlement, was that I felt sorry for Aristotle. He'd made some accurate observations and come close to a theory of evolution but gave it up as far-fetched.

Later on I got what the Great Books guy was up to. He meant that Aristotle saw the historical development of the genres of epic and tragedy as something like the growth of a plant. Aristotle does say in the *Poetics* "that tragedy grew over time, changing at least into its 'natural form.'"

Okay. There's the analogy to an oak tree starting from an acorn, germinating, shooting up, spreading its branches into a crown—and there it is in *its* attainment of its natural form. Very likely Aristotle was influenced by his own *Physics*. But he was aware of the difference between how trees grow and how humans invent stories. He praises his favorite writers; he also points out the mistakes some pretty good and some not so good writers have made. There was nothing preordained; *some* writers got it right. Aeschylus and Sophocles consciously adapted their stories to the stage, which had been music-hall stuff. A colleague of mine, Paul Cantor, wrote an essay on the subject. He says, "With Aeschylus and Sophocles poetry recaptured the elevated level of the Homeric epics, once more portraying noble action, but now with all the accumulated force of theatrical representation."

Even though human invention is informed by instincts for order and symmetry, there is choice, and there is an uneven distribution of the talent for invention.

I also think that Aristotle's remarks about wholeness, completeness, magnitude, and causality are constituents of what Aristotle felt as tragic pleasure. Pity and terror and then catharsis. Catharsis: purging, cleansing, purifying. It is not relief; it is not "there but for the grace of God go I." It means that the viewer's experience has been climactic. It has left one's psyche purified.

Aristotle doesn't use the phrase "willing suspension of disbelief" but something like it is implied. He says that tragedy isn't just about creating a unified whole. It is also necessary that the incidents create pity and fear in the audience. "Such an effect is best produced when the events come on us by surprise; and the effect is heightened when, at the same time they follow as cause and effect." Inevitable *and* surprising? A contradiction? The example of the end of *Oedipus the King* entwines inevitability and surprise. Doom is foretold; Oedipus' anguished reaction is painfully shocking.

Aristotle is being analytical, but when he says, "have the very greatest effect on the mind," it's fair to infer he's speaking of his own mind, of his own experience of tragic pleasure.

I THINK THESE pieces of the *Poetics* we've been considering are accurate Aristotle. I think that not just because they are insistently careful but also because they address the questions that still vex us—form and content, surprise and inevitability, fate and free will.

If you don't know Greek—I don't—the next best thing is to read several different translations. After you have some ideas of your own you might find a classical scholar, even the Great Books guy. I once asked a smart friend how he got smart. He said, "I argued with guys who were smarter. I got mowed down. That's how I got smarter." Maybe you can find some smarter people who are also nice, who mow you down gently.

Then go back to Aristotle. See if you also find that underneath it, it's not only analysis; he's saying how much he loves a good story.

THINGS

Instances of the right thing *being as important as the right word.*

O for a muse of fire, that would ascend
The brightest heaven of invention:
A kingdom for a stage, princes to act,
And monarchs to behold the swelling scene.
Then should the warlike Harry, like himself,
Assume the port of Mars, and at his heels,
Leashed in like hounds, should famine, sword and
    fire
Crouch for employment. But pardon, gentles all,
The flat unraisèd spirits that have dared
On this unworthy scaffold to bring forth
So great an object. Can this cockpit hold
The vasty fields of France? Or may we cram

Within this wooden O the very casques
That did affright the air at Agincourt?
O, pardon: since a crookèd figure may
Attest in little place, a million,
And let us, ciphers to this great accompt,
On your imaginary forces work.
Suppose within the girdle of these walls
Are now confined two mighty monarchies,
Whose high, uprearèd, and abutting fronts
The perilous narrow ocean parts asunder.
Pick out our imperfections with your thoughts;
Into a thousand parts divide one man,
And make imaginary puissance.
Think, when we talk of horses, that you see them
Printing their proud hooves i' th' receiving earth. . . .

—WILLIAM SHAKESPEARE, *Henry V,* act I, prologue

It's these last two lines—"Think, when we talk of horses that you see them / Printing their proud hooves i' th' receiving earth"—that I see most clearly, that I would like to follow in tight focus. Things. Things in motion. Things at work.

"The vasty fields of France" and "two mighty monarchies" are grand—grand is grand.

Writers are understandably eager to get to the part of the story where we get to talk about what it all feels like, what it all means, the thrill of dilated language. On the way there, there are *things.* How much do we need to know about how things work? How much prior knowledge can we assume our readers have? What is the point at which a narrative is impeded by too much how-to instruction?

From time to time the pendulum swings from "art for art"

to "go out with a notebook and pencil stub" . . . and then back again. To damp the swing toward things this note: A very good book on whaling is *Nimrod of the Sea*, by William Morris Davis, a nineteenth-century firsthand account and a general survey. It has more instruction, more events, more *things* than *Moby-Dick*. I would recommend *Nimrod of the Sea* for its information and historical interest. It does not provide as much narrative pleasure, nor as beautiful sentences, nor does it evoke pity or terror.

Take the one short passage in which Pip, the *Pequod*'s cabin boy falls overboard and is lost from sight. He is miraculously saved, but he's been terrified beyond measure by seeing nothing but ocean. Melville ends the incident with this: "The sea had jeeringly kept his finite body up, but drowned the infinite of his soul. He saw God's foot upon the treadle of the loom, and spoke it; and therefore his shipmates called him mad."

There was a time when there weren't so many things in the world that needed to be explained—or could be explained. Noah's ark. It's forty cubits long, made of gopher wood, and sealed with pitch. That's all. Not an instruction manual on how to build a boat. Not the point of the story anyway; the story's about God preserving a seed crop of people and other animals. And most of the audience had some idea of a boat.

For a long time the things in stories were familiar. Abraham's knife and ram. Ulysses's bow. Aaron's rod. Nero's fiddle (or lyre). Arthur's sword Excalibur. Roland's horn that sounded at Roncesvalles. William Tell's crossbow. When the rosy-fingered dawn broke, and the oars smote the wine-dark sea, no listener or reader needed an instruction manual.

It's not that there hadn't been wonderful inventions that figured in the plot of history, if not fiction. Claude Lévi-Strauss, in his brilliant and most readable book *Tristes tropiques*, remarks that the Neolithic Age was the most brilliant age of invention. The club, throwing sticks, flint arrowheads, spearheads, and knives; clothes; fibers twined into rope; the knot; rafts and boats; huts; the bow-drill method of making fire; pots; fishnets and fish weirs. In Siberia archaeologists have found skis that they figure are about twenty thousand years old. And who knows what ways they used all these things.

I don't want to fall into the mistake that some early anthropologists made—that is, to suppose modern-day isolated tribes using Stone Age tools are living the same life as Stone Age people. And yet . . .

Here is an ingenious way to hunt that requires only a big stick and a flat piece of rock for a shovel. When geese graze on land there is always one goose on sentry duty—head up, looking around, while the others are bent over in the grass. Sentry duty rotates. The predator appears, the sentry honks, and the geese fly away.

You find a field that geese feed in. Before they arrive, you dig a trench an inch deep at one end and two feet deep at the other. Make it a bit wider than a goose's body with folded wings but less wide than its wingspan. You strew the trench with whatever the geese are eating—say, grains of strand wheat, hulled to make them more tempting. You make the trail of grain sparse over the entrance, abundant at the deep end. You hide. The geese fly in for their morning meal. A goose begins to feed in the trench. When the goose reaches the deep end you run to it. The sentry honks. The geese spread their wings. All but one. That goose's wings are caught short by the sides of the trench.

A blow to the head with your stick. Perhaps because you don't want to bruise the meat. Or perhaps you want the goose to die instantly, perhaps because you revere geese, or perhaps because you've learned that animals that die slowly in pain and panic don't taste as good. You don't know the word *adrenaline*, but you have paid attention, or you have listened to your elders.

I heard this from Tom "Tracker" Brown, a survival instructor. He heard it from his Native American friend who heard it from his grandfather, who may have heard it from *his* grandfather. I don't know how many grandfathers might be in the chain.

In general the lives of nomadic peoples—their practices and stories—are unrecorded. This is in part because they use things made of hide or bone or wood, and those things, unlike cities of stone or clay tablets or metal tools, return to earth.

Think, when we talk of horses . . . think of riding a horse. The remnants of the earliest horse riding that survive are (1) the bit, which perhaps was bone or wood but at some point became metal, and (2) the stirrup. The stirrup was a terrible advance in technology because it gave an even firmer support to a rider thrusting with a lance or sword. "The Assyrian came down like a wolf on the fold / And his cohorts were gleaming in purple and gold."

The poet knew how to ride, everyone knew how to ride—the technology must have seemed to him to be part of the way things had always been.

History and story were mostly about the fate of people, about Providence.

The age of European exploration started, among other things, a sense of wonder. From the Renaissance through the eighteenth century, people made collections of wonders from newfound lands. And yet the exemplary (and wonderful-in-their-own-way) novels of the eighteenth century don't require much how-to. There is wit, sensation, and argument about Providence. Consider Laurence Sterne and his French literary kin Denis Diderot—*Jacques the Fatalist and His Master*. Brilliant, witty, ribald—but *things* are much as they've always been. Or *Tom Jones* or *Clarissa* or *Moll Flanders*.

Ah—in *Robinson Crusoe* Daniel Defoe does include a lot of things and how to use them. So there is that little island.

But it isn't until the Industrial Revolution that there is the great outpouring of things, made possible by the steam engine and mills and factories. Things are manufactured faster and faster and are shipped faster and faster by rail, by sailing ships faster and larger than ever, and eventually steamships. Cities—seaports, manufacturing centers, commercial centers—grow and grow. A simple and incomplete explanation is the extraordinary confluence of science, invention, and commerce. There are many consequences, but one is—to pick a manageable but representative group—Charles Dickens, Honoré de Balzac, Émile Zola.

Dickens had a friend named Henry Mayhew. The two of them walked and walked around London, I imagine, pointing out things to each other. Mayhew wrote a number of works, still in print today, usually collected under the title *London Cheaters and Crooks.* Mayhew was a pioneer sociologist, noting hundreds of new occupations, some honest, some not. He moralizes a bit, but he is exact in the details of the new tools of each trade, of the way workers' lives are formed or deformed by their new employments.

I'm not saying Dickens rode piggyback on Mayhew. I imagine rather that they were catalysts to each other. Dickens noted the new trades, the new social network that emerged, but also gave voice to the heretofore unlikely aspirations of the middle class, he himself a case in point—from blacking factory to world fame.

Balzac. A country boy come to Paris—which is part of the plot of *Le père Goriot* (*Father Goriot*), *Lost Illusions, Cousine Bette* (*Cousin Bette*), and many of the other novels in *The Human Comedy*. But he is also a chronicler of things. A way to measure this: If you read French at a college level you can understand Jean Racine, Pierre Corneille, Jean-Jacques Rousseau, Claude Prosper Jolyot de Crébillon, and pretty much learn the vocabulary. The first chapters of *Lost Illusions*, however, will send you to the dictionary—there is *everything* about the manufacture of roof tiles. In *César Birotteau* there is everything about the perfume trade, and that has its special vocabulary. There are two reasons for all this realistic detail. Enterprise is the social springboard for the ambitious. The success of a character in an enterprise *is* his character. (Women in Balzac have key roles, but the trajectory of their lives is treated differently.) The other reason for realistic detail is that a character marks his rise or fall by things: Are his clothes à la mode? To what degree of luxury is his house furnished? His rival's house? His mistress's house?

A grad student once complained that he thought Balzac did low life convincingly—think of the boarding house in *Le père Goriot*—but that the descriptions of the houses and rooms of the haut monde seemed to be written by some arriviste daydreaming over a catalog. I said, "You insolent pup . . ." No, I didn't. It is true that Balzac in his real life had the taste of, say, Donald Trump. But what rings true is when one of Balzac's characters on the make enters a grand house. The character at first goes into a fragile state of admiration and envy but is also able to tell the difference between an established noblewoman's taste and the creamier luxury of the wife of a recently titled banker, or the extravagance of an actress maintained by a rich man.

Something else happens as the Industrial Revolution gets up its full head of steam. But before we get to Zola, a brief footnote on the ownership of things. John Locke (a century and some earlier) wrote that a workman's tools—a farmer's horse and plow, a carpenter's saw and drill, a weaver's loom—are extensions of the person. Locke was giving a moral justification of ownership. (He also wrote that no one should own more land than a person could till, but he changed course on that, saying that money was in effect stored-up labor, so it's okay for someone to own lots of land since that person is tilling it with stored-up labor.)

The individual was still the subject of Locke's reflections; the individual was still the subject of stories.

But by the time the nineteenth century ripened, many industrial workers became cogs of a larger mechanism made up of machines and workers. The enterprise, whether employing factory workers, sandhogs, miners, or department store clerks, becomes a force of its own. The workers don't own the tools—rather, the tools own them. *Mechanization Takes Command.* (That is the title, by the way, of an amazing book by a Swiss historian of technology, Sigfried Giedion. It's out of print but about to come back in, and rightly so. One of his observations is that slaughterhouse workers in mass production are apt to become less sensitive to other people's pain or death.)

The opening scene in Zola's *Germinal* (the name of the first month of spring in the French revolutionary calendar) is not technical. A solitary figure is walking across a cold wind-swept plain at night, looking for shelter, food, a job. It is tedious—and the writing is harsh and good. The walker finds a village—or rather a new mining town. It has no name; it has a number.

> Étienne stood for a moment, deafened and blinded, and chilled to the bone by the draughts coming from every direction. Then he moved forward a few paces, drawn by the gleaming steel and brass of the winding-engine . . .

And now Zola does have to get technical because very few of his readers have seen a "modern" mine. There follows a description of the machinery that lower men, children, and horses into the pit. There are lots of numbers: horsepower, diameter of wheels, length of the main cable, how many miners per elevator cage, and so forth. Zola visited such a mine. I assume that he took notes and in his "naturalist" enthusiasm for precise detail he put the facts and figures in. Occasionally there is a more impressionistic sentence:

> One thing Étienne did grasp: the pit could swallow people in mouthfuls of twenty or thirty at a time and with such ease that it seemed not even to notice the moment of their consumption . . .
>
> "Is it a long way down?" Étienne asked a sleepy-looking miner.
>
> "Five-hundred and fifty-four metres."
>
> They both fell silent, gazing at the cable . . .
>
> "And what if that breaks?"
>
> "Ah well, if that breaks . . ."

This passage is exact in its instructive measurements, but it also begins to give some resonance to the mine as a character in the novel. As the story goes on, it becomes clearer that the mine controls the lives not only of the miners but also of the foremen, engineers, managers, and owners.

The risk is pathetic fallacy—the mine as an eater of men, women, boys and girls. Even children go down in the pits. Zola does not attribute human agency to the mine—but it is more than a stage on which the novel's humans contest their wishes. The mine is a confluence of natural forces—of geologic faults, water, and gas; of human invention—the machinery to extract coal; and of human investment for profit and desperate human labor.

Étienne becomes a miner. It doesn't take a stroke of genius to have character start with a blank slate, but it's a good idea to have him learn so we can learn along with him. This, by the way, is how Patrick O'Brian is able to pass along the details of seamanship necessary to his series of novels about the British navy during the Napoleonic Wars. One of the main characters, Stephen Maturin, is the doctor on board. He is a linguist, zoologist, and an intelligence agent, but he doesn't know beans about a sailing ship. Captain Jack Aubrey is astounded at his ignorance, teases him, and fills him in as necessary.

When is the best time to tell people how something works? When they really need to know. Some of the best instruction on rock climbing is given at Outward Bound Schools. The instructor says nothing—well, almost nothing—until you're halfway up the cliff. At that point, most people are all ears.

So at first Étienne is our conduit, he being, so to speak, halfway up the cliff. Or down. Information in almost undiluted block form isn't necessary later on. We've got all we need to know bit by bit in incident after incident. Now that we've seen the shaft and know the ropes, we can get more, and more efficiently.

More horses. These live out their life down in the mine, pulling carts of coal.

> ... and they were bringing a horse down, which was always an anxious moment because occasionally the animal would be so terrified that it would be dead on arrival. Up on the surface it would struggle wildly as they wrapped it in a net; then, as it felt the ground vanish from under its feet, it would go quite still, petrified with fear ... This particular horse had been too big to fit and they had been obliged to tie its head back against its flanks.
>
> Finally he appeared, as motionless as stone, his eyes dilated with terror. It was a bay, hardly three years old, called Trumpet.

Soon Trumpet was lying in a heap on the cast-iron floor . . . They were beginning to untie him when [the old horse] Battle . . . came over and stretched out his neck to sniff this new companion . . .

What lovely smell was that?

[Battle] must have caught the scent of good fresh air and the long-forgotten smell of sun-drenched grass . . .

At the top nothing had shifted . . . But when he reached the lower tubbing at a depth of three hundred metres his head lamp went out just as he had foreseen: a spurt of water . . . From then on he could see only by the light of the lamp underneath . . . Only a few timber staves in the tubbing remained; the others had disappeared along with their frames. Behind them yawned huge cavities from which yellow sand, as fine as flour, was pouring out . . . while the waters of the Torrent, that forgotten underground sea with its own storms and wrecks, were gushing forth as though from an open sluice . . . The further he descended the louder grew the screaming . . . an impassable obstacle was blocking the shaft: a pile of tubbing staves, the broken beams of the cage-rails and the shattered remains of the escape-shaft partitions all lay in a tangled mass . . . the screaming suddenly stopped.

For all his sympathy for the miners Zola is not easy on them. *Germinal* is not melodrama with simple good guys on the one hand and irredeemably bad guys on the other. I'm not giving away much when I say there's a strike. What's realistic about that part of the plot is the diversity of opinion, the confusion, the fits and starts of the leaders' theories, and the uncontrollable movement of the workers once they get started.

Zola's description of the miners' sex lives is like Hobbes's description of life in general—nasty, brutish, and short.

Zola in a letter (italics added) wrote:

> Perhaps this time they'll stop seeing me as someone who insults the people. Is not the true socialist he who describes their poverty and wretchedness and the ways in which they are remorselessly dragged down, who shows the prison-house of hunger in all its horror? Those who extol the blessedness of the people are mere elegists who should be consigned to history along with the humanitarian claptrap of 1848. If the people are so perfect and divine, why try and improve their lot? No, the people are downtrodden, in ignorance and mire, and *it is from that ignorance and that mire that we should endeavor to raise them.*

This passage is both a political stance and an additional explanation and justification of literary realism.

Evidently the miners agreed. Zola was famous and, in certain quarters, infamous for his defense of Captain Alfred Dreyfus—a defense that at last showed Dreyfus was wrongly convicted, a victim of the anti-Semitism of certain army officers. When Zola died "50,000 people followed the funeral procession through the streets of Paris, including a delegation of miners." The miners "chanted . . . 'Germinal! Germinal! Germinal!'"

The Perfect Storm by Sebastian Junger is another book whose emotional impact is heightened by exact, even technical physical description. The crucial part of this book isn't fiction, but it's not entirely nonfiction. Nobody knows what happened to the swordfishing boat *Andrea Gail.* Junger faithfully records the last radio contacts. He quotes the firsthand accounts of seamen on other ships who barely escaped when their ships pitch-poled or rolled and ended up upside down. He quotes the accounts of other captains and crewmembers who were in the same storm but by good fortune not in the same spot the *Andrea Gail* was in. He gives a good account of how waves are formed: (1) wind speed, (2) how long the wind blows, and (3) "fetch"—the length of open water across which the winds blow and in which waves are formed. "All waves no matter how huge start as rough spots—'cats' paws'—on the surface of the water. The cats' paws are filled with diamond-shaped ripples, called capillary waves . . . They give the wind some purchase on an otherwise glassy sea . . . The harder the wind blows, the bigger the waves get and the more water they are able to 'catch.' It's a feedback loop that has wave height rising exponentially with wind speed."

From the weather service, Junger learns the wind speeds and wave heights around the last reported position of the *Andrea Gail*. Wind: 120 mph. Peak waves: one hundred feet. He then must imagine what happened.

Whether the *Andrea Gail* rolls, pitch-poles or gets driven down, she winds up, one way or another, in a position from which she cannot recover. Among marine architects this is known as the zero-moment point—the point of no return. The transition from crisis to catastrophe is fast, probably under a minute, or someone would have tripped the EPIRB [emergency position-indicating radio beacon] . . . There's no time to put on survival suits or grab a life vest; the boat's moving through the most extreme motion of her life and there isn't even time to shout. The refrigerator comes out of the wall and crashes across the galley. Dirty dishes cascade out of the sink. The TV, the washing machine . . . the men, all go flying. And seconds later the water moves in.

When a boat floods, the first thing that happens is that her electrical system shorts out. The lights go off and for a few moments the only illumination is the frenetic blue of sparks arcing down into the water . . .

After that the water rises up the companionway, flooding the galley and berths, and then starts up the inverted engine room hatch . . . If the boat is hull-up and there are men in the engine room, they are the last to die.

At this point Junger does something odd, even shocking. He stops his narration of what is happening to the boat and brings in what is essentially a cold medical text.

The instinct not to breathe underwater is so strong that it overcomes the agony of running out of air. No matter how desperate the drowning person is, he doesn't inhale until he's on the verge of losing consciousness. At that point there's so much carbon dioxide in the blood, and so little oxygen, that chemical sensors in the brain trigger an involuntary breath whether he's underwater or not. That is called the "break point." . . . It's a sort of neurological optimism, as if the body were saying, *Holding our breath is killing us, and breathing in might not kill us, so we might as well breathe in . . .*

When the first involuntary breath occurs most people are still conscious, which is unfortunate, because the only thing more unpleasant than running out of air is breathing in water . . .

Water floods the lungs and ends any waning transfer of oxygen to the blood . . . [H]alf-conscious and enfeebled by oxygen depletion the person is in no position to fight his way back up to the surface. The very process of drowning makes

it harder and harder not to drown, [a] disaster curve similar
to that of a sinking boat.

It is with that last phrase that we leave the tight focus of how a
body drowns and once again see the *Andrea Gail*. We have read
how waves work (there's a good deal more that I've left out),
we've read about the zero-moment point (there's also a good
deal more), and we get a general narrative— "When a boat
floods . . ."—but we know it's the *Andrea Gail*. Just as we know
that the lungs that are filling are those of the captain and crew
of the *Andrea Gail*. Junger fills in a last detail.

> The central nervous system does not know what has hap-
> pened to the body; all it knows is that not enough oxygen is
> getting to the brain. Orders are still being issued—*Breathe!*
> *Pump! Circulate!*—that the body cannot obey . . . still the
> body is doing everything it can to delay the inevitable . . .
>
> The electrical activity in their brain gets weaker and weaker
> until, after fifteen or twenty minutes, it ceases altogether.

And then Junger underlines a parallel he's set up earlier: "The
body could be likened to a crew that resorts to increasingly desperate measures to keep their vessel afloat . . . [T]he last wire has
shorted out, the last bit of decking has settled under the water."
It is now that Junger writes the names, names that we grew
used to during the voyage out, during the setting of the lines,
during their first anxiety about the storm: ". . . the last bit of
decking has settled under the water. Tyne, Pierre, Sullivan,
Moran, Murphy, and Shatford are dead."
The Perfect Storm is the only book I've listened to on tape. I was
driving from Chicago to Iowa City. Halfway through the med-

ical description of how a body drowns, I had to pull over. Good move, because when I heard the names I involuntarily curled up in a spasm.

I don't think I would have without the carefully built enumeration of things: the boat herself, the antenna blown away, the EPIRB, the survival suits, the wiring for the radio and lights— all the details of how things work, are supposed to work and stop working when the boat turns over, floods, and goes down.

In retrospect, I'm struck that an instructive medical passage—something that in another context I might have noted with detached interest—led to the moment of greatest pity and terror.

SEX AND VIOLENCE

Is "less is more" the best advice about writing sex scenes? Less of what? And what's more?

Also some thoughts about cathexis, both as a psychiatric term and as a metaphor.

(I don't get to violence. But in A Sentimental Journey through France and Italy, *Laurence Sterne never gets to Italy.)*

'VE LEARNED a lot from students: sometimes what to do, sometimes what not. Long ago a student handed in a story with a sex scene at the end. The sex was lengthy and active. There was play-by-play description as well as color commentary, something like Howard Cosell and Don Gifford announcing *Monday Night Football*. I lost any sense of who the characters were, perhaps because the characters had lost any sense of who they were. I didn't know enough at the time to point that out. In conference, I asked the writer if she wanted to have the story discussed in workshop. "Oh no," she said. "I wouldn't want anyone to read it." That put us at ease. I wasn't anyone; I was a reading machine, so I gave a mechanical response. I said, "Sometimes less is more."

WHAT I DIDN'T know then my friend and adviser, Tony Winner, hinted at a bit later. I'd written a story in which a woman, to distract herself from a difficult situation, takes her dog for a walk in the woods. The dog chases a rabbit, the woman runs after the dog. A patchy fog blows in. The woman can't find the trail. She panics. Runs. Trips. Does all the things a person lost in the woods shouldn't do. Tony said, "I like the beginning. I had a sense of the woman. I liked the ending. I had another sense of her. The lost-in-the-woods part was just an account of being lost in the woods."

I thought about that. What he didn't say—what he left to me to figure out—is that in moments of great physical pain or fear or of great physical pleasure any one of us is momentarily simplified to a yowl or a yelp. Okay. But no need to go on and on about the yowl.

Years later I heard a lecture by my colleague Jane Alison. She quoted a passage from *The Nature of Narrative* by Robert Scholes and Robert Kellogg, the pith of which is "Quality of mind . . . not plot, is the soul of narrative."

My own earlier formulation is: plot is the nutcracker, which opens the shell of a character so that we can sense the inmost savor. (Whenever I say this, I smell a just opened almond. Mild synesthesia.)

I think the two Bobs, Jane, and I are on the same page.

I don't think Aristotle is in direct opposition when he ranks "actions" as more important than "character" in his list of the elements of a good tragedy.

AT ABOUT THE same time as the first story with the long sex-scene ending, I got another story from a student. Also boy/girl, as many undergraduate stories tend to be. Conversation at restaurant. Some hint of attraction. But the boy isn't sure. They leave the restaurant, start to cross a busy street. She holds him back by the hem of his sleeve as a car passes by. She laughs. She leads him across the street. She lets go but then turns, smiles, and takes his sleeve again.

I wish I could remember the exact words, but in a way it's pleasing to remember only the sense of the paragraph. To see the picture but, more important, to sense the girl's fingers on the boy's sleeve and, above all, to sense his sensation.

To THE FIRST writer, Russell Banks might've said, as he in fact did say in an interview as general advice: "We know about the physiology. What a writer needs to tell us in a sex scene are the things we don't know." And to underline that point: A friend of mine was listening to CSPAN and he heard an economist testifying before a congressional subcommittee. How the economist brought this anecdote into policy discussions, I don't know, but apparently a friend of his from Cincinnati won a free trip to Paris, the whole shebang—he got a hotel suite, tickets to the opera. He got back to Cincinnati and his friends took him to lunch at their golf club, and they said, How was Paris? Excellent, he said. Outstanding opera, the museums . . . No, they said, come on. How was Par*ee*? Okay, he said, I did meet this truly elegant French woman at the Louvre; we had coffee at a café—you know how French coffee has that peculiar tang—and then dinner, and then she asked me back to her place, an apartment on the Left Bank, and I smelled her perfume and asked about it, and she showed me how Frenchwomen put on perfume, a dab behind the ear, just another dot between the breasts and a slightly larger dot high on the inner thigh. The man stopped. His friends said, Yeah, yeah, and what about the rest? The man said, The rest was just the same as in Cincinnati.

THE RUSSELL BANKS remark is from a book called *The Joy of Writing Sex* by Elizabeth Benedict. A point of disclosure: I was surprised to find that I'd been interviewed and cited. I'd certainly talked with her; I'd known her since she was the babysitter for my nephews. And I'd read all her novels, but I'd skipped *The Joy of Writing Sex* because I didn't like the title—I thought it was kind of a silly tie-in to *The Joy of Sex*, a now-forgotten sex manual. But I did finally read it because I heard Margot Livesey recommend it as one of the better books on how to write fiction in general. I found myself agreeing with almost all the points that Liz Benedict and her interviewees make even though they contradict each other, because sometimes more is less and sometimes less is more and sometimes more is more. But all in all it's a good survey of writing fiction in general and attitudes about sex in fiction as they change from the 1950s to the '60s and on to the end of the last century.

JOHN UPDIKE WROTE to Liz Benedict that he doesn't enjoy sex scenes of other writers as much as he enjoys his own. He also said, "Writing my sex scenes physically excites me, as it should," and added, "The trick is, of course, once sex is not off limits, is to keep it from being boring and to make it continuous with the book's psychology and symbolism elsewhere."

RUSSELL BANKS IS more self-restricting. "When I first began writing I was less clear about the difference between writing and fantasizing and so when I wrote about sex I tended to have a sexual fantasy. It took a while to realize that wasn't doing anyone any good, not even me, and it wasn't doing the writing any good. And I began to realize I had to approach it with the same attention to craft and to function as I did with every other scene."

AND THEN MY favorite, from Deborah Eisenberg:

> The anatomical possibilities are limited, so a poorly written sex scene can be a little like hearing an eight-year-old describe the plot of his favorite movie. And on the other hand, because every reader brings to every sex scene *vivid* prior experience, writing graphically about sex can also be a little like writing: *dead mother.* You'll get a response, all right, but it might not be the response you want, or the response that proceeds from all the careful work you've done to show exactly what's happening between these two particular people—or these twelve particular people—right now. The hazard is that if you, the writer, are insufficiently in control, the response you'll get is the one that the reader would have had to any sex scene whatsoever that came his or her way. The problems of cliché and generality, which are exactly what writing is a battle against, are especially hard to outwit when you're writing about sex because the reader's response is so likely to be automatic and blinding. It's as if a flash were

going off, obscuring all the specifics and detail and nuance you've constructed so carefully about your characters and their encounter. Of course, that's the way sex sometimes works in real life—you know: Well, I actually don't happen to care just now *who* that person is—and if that's what you want, fine.

I've been somewhat more interested in the thwarted impulse—the erotic charge inappropriately pervading all sorts of experience. One of the most sexually interesting scenes in literature is in *Anna Karenina* when Vronsky returns to his barracks after seeing Anna, and his roommate tells him an absolutely idiotic, very funny anecdote about helmets. Anna isn't in the scene at all—she's far away—but you're very aware of her. The uncanny giddiness you experience along with Vronsky has to do, I think, with the shift in sexual power between Anna and him at that moment; the erotic obsession is like an animal that's released Vronsky temporarily, to settle its entire weight on Anna. The sexuality that's collapsed into that scene with the roommate is just so complex—and intense, and accurate, and *specific*.

THAT LAST PART of Deborah Eisenberg's remarks reminded me of a word that is, I think, the way out of the perhaps false dilemma of whether less is more or more is less. And the word is *cathexis*. It's a word from a psychiatrist's vocabulary, though I first heard it from a friend who was criticizing a story of mine. He said, "Johnny, it's not fully cathected."

The online *Free Dictionary* definition is "concentration of emotional energy on an object or idea. Additionally, the libidinal energy invested in some idea or person or object." Freud thought of cathexis as a psychic analog of an electric charge. I didn't know all that then, so I asked my friend what the word meant. He wandered through the psychiatric stuff, but then he added: It means full to the brim. And what I saw then and what sticks in my mind is a glass so full that the water is above the rim but kept in place by surface tension. I then somehow turned this picture idea into something happening between two people. I imagined the air thickening between the two, the space between them becoming a condensed and urgent medium.

THE FIRST STUDENT story I brought up (the one with the lengthy sex scene, the tearing off of clothes and thrashing around) is action without cathexis. The second is action with cathexis, although it is very slight action—the girl taking the boy by the sleeve. He didn't know what she was thinking, but he was fully concentrated, fully invested in finding out. Her gesture was in three parts: (1) saving him from car; (2) leading him across the street—perhaps teasingly; and (3) now that she's been a crossing guard and his mommy, touching him in a way that has "libidinal energy."

THE EMOTIONAL ENERGY, the libidinal energy, can be of many kinds, even combinations, even contradictory combinations: desire, fear, repugnance, desperation, curiosity, malice.

In a very good D. H. Lawrence story called "The Horse Dealer's Daughter," there is cathexis with four or five variations. It's a case of more is more. There are more sentences than there are actual seconds of time in the crucial scene. Like the impending kiss in *Remembrance of Things Past*, when Marcel is bending toward a girl in a hotel room and she idly reaches up to ring the call-the-waiter bell. The Proust passage goes on for a page. It includes an essay on art, and how if you look at certain paintings in the Sistine Chapel they invert, as Albertine's head appears to invert. The last sentence is "Albertine rang the bell." It's a wonderful expansion of time. Cathexis doesn't mean explaining, although Proust is explaining a lot, *by the way*. The cathexis is in the built-up yearning. The passage comes from the volume of *Remembrance of Things Past* titled "Within a Budding Grove." The original French is "À l'ombre des jeunes filles en fleurs" ("In the Shadow of Young Girls in Bloom"). In "The Horse Dealer's Daughter" the scene takes only a few minutes in the characters' lives during which they speak only a few sentences, but Lawrence describes—evokes—what is invisible and inaudible in a fierce five pages.

WHAT PRECEDES THE final scene is a steady setup. A horse farm has gone broke. The three brothers are watching the horses being trotted off.

> The great draught-horses swung past. They were tied head to tail, four of them, and they heaved along to where a lane branched off from the high-road, planting their great hoofs floutingly in the fine black mud, swinging their great rounded haunches sumptuously, and trotting a few sudden steps as they were led into the lane.

LAWRENCE OFTEN BEGINS his stories with something physically impressive. A huge steam locomotive begins "Odor of Chrysanthemums"; a cavalry regiment on the move begins "The Prussian Officer." These scenes of animal or mechanical energy are preludes to the stories of the equally powerful energy passing between two humans.

The horse dealers' sister, who has been keeping house for them since the father died, is silent while her brothers brag and tease to cover their forlornness. A hint of what is inside her comes when a young doctor drops by.

"What are *you* going to do, then, Miss Pervin?" asked Fergusson. "Going to your sister's, are you?"

Mabel looked at him with her steady, dangerous eyes, that always made him uncomfortable . . .

Everybody leaves.

Mabel goes to tend her mother's grave. The doctor watches her from his neighboring property. "She seemed so intent and remote, it was like looking into another world."

Some time later he watches her walk toward a deep pond, then into it. In the dusk he loses sight of her. He runs to the pond, wades in. Finds her under the water. He pulls her out— "He lifted her and staggered onto the bank, out of the horror of wet, grey clay."

He takes her into the house, unconscious. He takes off her wet clothes, wraps her in a blanket. He drinks a shot of whisky and puts some in her mouth.

The effect was instantaneous. She looked full into his face, as if she had been seeing him for some time, and yet had only just become conscious of him.

"Dr. Fergusson?" she said.

"What?" he answered.

He was divesting himself of his coat, intending to find some dry clothing upstairs. He could not bear the smell of the dead, clayey water, and he was mortally afraid for his own health.

"What did I do?" she asked.

"Walked into the pond," he replied. He had begun to shudder like one sick, and could hardly attend to her. Her eyes remained full on him, he seemed to be going dark in his mind, looking back at her helplessly. The shuddering became quieter in him, his life came back to him, dark and unknowing, but strong again.

Lawrence believed in something like Henri Bergson's *élan vital*—*élan* means "impulse," "surge," "momentum"—and *vital*, as in English, means "living" and "essential." *Élan vital* is often translated as "life force." For Bergson, it was wonderful and positive. For Lawrence, it was wonderful but fearsome. It could shake a modern civilized man to pieces. It also, in Lawrence's view, arises in a different form in women than in men. Most of Lawrence's male characters aren't as prepared to be possessed by it.

"Was I out of my mind?" she asked, while her eyes were fixed on him all the time.

"Maybe, for the moment,' he replied. He felt quiet, because his strength had come back. The strange fretful strain had left him.

"Am I out of my mind now?" she asked.

"Are you?" He reflected a moment. "No," he answered truthfully. "I don't see that you are." He turned his face aside. He was afraid now, because he felt dazed, and felt dimly that her power was stronger than his, in this issue. And she continued to look at him fixedly all the time. "Can you tell me where I shall find some dry things to put on?" he asked.

"Did you dive into the pond for me?" she asked.

"No," he answered. "I walked in. But I went in overhead as well."

There was silence for a moment. He hesitated. He very much wanted to go upstairs to get into dry clothing. But there was another desire in him. And she seemed to hold him. His will seemed to have gone to sleep, and left him, standing there slack before her. But he felt warm inside himself. He did not shudder at all, though his clothes were sodden on him.

"Why did you?" she asked.

"Because I didn't want you to do such a foolish thing," he said.

"It wasn't foolish," she said, still gazing at him as she lay on the floor, with a sofa cushion under her head. "It was the right thing to do. *I* knew best, then."

"I'll go and shift these wet things," he said. But still he had not the power to move out of her presence, until she sent him. It was as if she had the life of his body in her hands, and he could not extricate himself. Or perhaps he did not want to.

Suddenly she sat up. Then she became aware of her own immediate condition. She felt the blankets about her, she knew her own limbs. For a moment it seemed as if her reason were going. She looked round, with wild eye, as if seeking something. He stood still with fear. She saw her clothing lying scattered.

"Who undressed me?" she asked.

He only stood and stared at her, fascinated. His soul seemed to melt.

She shuffled forward on her knees, and put her arms round him, round his legs, as he stood there, pressing her breasts against his knees and thighs, clutching him with strange, convulsive certainty, pressing his thighs against her, drawing him to her face, her throat, as she looked up at him with flaring, humble eyes of transfiguration, triumphant in first possession.

"You love me," she murmured, in strange transport, yearning and triumphant and confident. "You love me. I know you love me, I know."

And she was passionately kissing his knees, through the wet clothing, passionately and indiscriminately kissing his knees, his legs, as if unaware of everything.

He looked down at the tangled wet hair, the wild, bare, animal shoulders. He was amazed, bewildered, and afraid. He had never thought of loving her. He had never wanted to love her. When he rescued her and restored her, he was a doctor, and she was a patient. He had had no single personal thought of her. Nay, this introduction of the personal element was very distasteful to him, a violation of his professional honour. It was horrible to have her there embracing his knees. It was horrible. He revolted from it, violently. And yet—and yet—he had not the power to break away.

She looked at him again, with the same supplication of powerful love, and that same transcendent frightening light of triumph. In view of the delicate flame which seemed to come from her face like a light, he was powerless. And yet he had never intended to love her. He had never intended. And something stubborn in him could not give way.

"You love me," she repeated, in a murmur of deep, rhapsodic assurance. "You love me."

Her hands were drawing him, drawing him down to her. He was afraid, even a little horrified. For he had, really, no intention of loving her. Yet her hands were drawing him towards her. He put out his hand quickly to steady himself, and grasped her bare shoulder. A flame seemed to burn the hand that grasped her soft shoulder. He had no intention of loving her: his whole will was against his yielding. It was horrible. And yet wonderful was the touch of her shoulders, beautiful the shining of her face. Was she perhaps mad? He had a horror of yielding to her. Yet something in him ached also.

He had been staring away at the door, away from her. But his hand remained on her shoulder. She had gone suddenly very still. He looked down at her. Her eyes were now wide with fear, with doubt, the light was dying from her face, a shadow of terrible greyness was returning. He could not bear the touch of her eyes' question upon him, and the look of death behind the question.

For all that Fergusson is a doctor with medical authority on his side, Mabel Pervin has mortal experience. When Mabel asked him why he saved her, Fergusson, trying to bring both her and him back to "normal," said, "Because I didn't want you to do such a foolish thing." She answered, "It wasn't foolish . . . It was the right thing to do. *I* knew best, then." She refuses his word *foolish*; she refuses to be his patient. She has been near death and is intent on the life she is beginning, fixing on Fergusson as simply as a newborn and as fully as a grown woman.

With an inward groan he gave way, and let his heart yield towards her. A sudden gentle smile came on his face. And her eyes, which never left his face, slowly, slowly filled with tears. He watched the strange water rise in her eyes, like some slow fountain coming up. And his heart seemed to burn and melt away in his breast.

He could not bear to look at her any more. He dropped on his knees and caught her head with his arms and pressed her face against his throat. She was very still. His heart, which seemed to have broken, was burning with a kind of agony in his breast. And he felt her slow, hot tears wetting his throat. But he could not move.

He felt the hot tears wet his neck and the hollows of his neck, and he remained motionless, suspended through one of man's eternities. Only now it had become indispensable to him to have her face pressed close to him; he could never let her go again. He could never let her head go away from the close clutch of his arm. He wanted to remain like that for ever, with his heart hurting him in a pain that was also life to him. Without knowing, he was looking down on her damp, soft brown hair.

Then, as it were suddenly, he smelt the horrid stagnant smell of that water. And at the same moment she drew away from him and looked at him. Her eyes were wistful and unfathomable. He was afraid of them, and he fell to kissing her, not knowing what he was doing. He wanted her eyes not to have that terrible, wistful, unfathomable look.

When she turned her face to him again, a faint delicate flush was glowing, and there was again dawning that terrible shining of joy in her eyes, which really terrified him, and yet which he now wanted to see, because he feared the look of doubt still more.

"You love me?" she said, rather faltering.

"Yes." The word cost him a painful effort. Not because it wasn't true. But because it was too newly true, the *saying* seemed to tear open again his newly-torn heart. And he hardly wanted it to be true, even now.

There used to be a debate, perhaps there still is, about whether Lawrence wrote "well." If by *well* the appraiser meant "elegantly" or "with easy grace," the answer was "not so much," and the appraiser pointed to repetitions, overinsistence, and awkwardness. (However, the early passage about the draught-horses is simply gorgeous—it echoes, consciously or unconsciously, the prologue to *Henry V*: "Think, when we talk of horses, that you see them / Printing their proud hoofs i' th' receiving earth.")

There are other passages in Lawrence that are crowded, the words elbowing each other in their rush to be heard. Some readers find these passages awkwardly headlong. Others find them powerful renditions of charged moments, perhaps headlong, but that's because the characters' senses are being overwhelmed. It's not "imitative fallacy;" it's not writing out the speech of a boring person going on too long. The characters are being overwhelmed in a new way with each new paragraph. There is a veering back and forth between physical action and emotion, between reason and instinct, each time with new reverberations.

Peter Taylor loved Lawrence's stories. He didn't like *Lady Chatterley's Lover* at all—"nothing but a sex manual." In the stories he found the fuller context of Lawrence's versions of eros, the other dimensions of full psychic engagement.

"THE SORCERER'S APPRENTICE" by Frank O'Connor has sex at its core, but it's not a story that's likely to inflame anyone's senses—unless it's a sense of humor. Not that it's laugh-out-loud funny; it's witty. It would take too long to summarize the twists of plot and attitudes. What interests me here is the distance from which Frank O'Connor writes the story. Una McDermott has been somewhat engaged to Jimmy Foley for five years. It is an Irish engagement such as they existed as recently as the late 1940s and early '50s, which is to say that Una is a thirty-year-old virgin. There is a supporting cast who follows the ups and downs of Una and Jimmy—"Their friends said that whenever Jimmy Foley named the day, Una McDermott slipped a disc." The slipped disc is a metaphor for Una picking a quarrel and going off to see her friends in Dublin, a married couple. The wife is alternately sympathetic and chiding. "When Una stayed with them, Joan got into Una's bed and they lay awake half the night, discussing every problem of love and marriage in the most concrete terms. Joan had been a nurse, so she knew all the terms."

The point of view is omniscient, hovering above the scene. The day-by-day, then minute-by-minute account starts when Denis, a forty-five-year-old cheerful and plump friend of the family comes to dinner. He becomes Una's new confidant. Una enjoys being charmed and charming. "Charm came natural to Una . . . When she wanted to be charming she could knock a man out in the first round."

There are some more swirls and spins—Joan is afraid for Una, then afraid for Denis, and everyone gets on edge. At what seems to be a moment of calm, "[Una] rang him up to invite him for a walk. Now that she had the situation in hand, she saw no reason why they should not be friends."

Okay. O'Connor comes down from on high to read Una's mind, though that last sentence flavored by Una's mind is a setup for the very next abrupt sentence: "At midnight she found herself in bed with him, lying in a most extraordinary position . . . God, she felt, could never have intended anything as absurd as this . . . What a dozen men with ten times his attraction had failed to do, he had managed without the slightest difficulty." That's it for the sex scene. "At one o'clock Denis was fast asleep and snoring, and somehow the snoring struck as far more compromising than anything that had happened before."

There is another sex scene the next week. Una goes back to her hometown, finds that Denis's advice about how to get along with her fiancé is sound. She then goes to a seaside inn with Jimmy. "When he said good-night to her in her room, she asked in a low voice: 'Aren't you going to stay with me, Jimmy?' He grew very red. 'Are you sure you want me to?' he replied. For answer, she turned her back on him and pulled her frock over her head."

She has a marvelous time; as far as she can tell Jimmy does too. Next morning, however, he's completely dressed when she wakes up. He can't look at her; his voice is far away. They quarrel again. She is stricken by her secret; he's stricken by the thought they've ruined themselves by doing something wrong.

> She began to sob, pulling wildly at her hair. "Oh, I'm a fool. I do my best, but I don't know anything. And you're right. It is awful."
>
> "Not awful," he said, weeping. "It's just that it's not the right thing for us."

Jimmy is out the door.

> The morning light brightened her room and revealed to her her own wickedness and folly. . . .
> Yet, even while she wept, she seemed to see Denis, his plump face aglow with good-natured laughter.

Next stop a pay phone and a call to Denis.

It's not Mabel Pervin's life force, but it's Una's—bit by bit after all the narrator's distant descriptions of Una's liveliness and haplessness, O'Connor's puckishness—"What fools these mortals be!"—gives way. O'Connor describes Una's morning-after hope, bewilderment, "tearing her hair wildly," and picking herself up again in more detail and with more alert sympathy than he gives to the sex scenes with Denis and Jimmy. The implication is there's more resilience in Una than resignation. The subtext is something like this: "Ah, Una—you're better off. You're well rid of a handsome stick, and you'll be right as rain with a man who gets your jokes. And anything else you'll tell him."

THE SEX SCENE—*scenes*—IN the last forty-five pages of *Ulysses* are all in Molly Bloom's memory and fantasy. Leopold Bloom is present physically. He is lying in bed, his head to her toes, but he is chiefly present in her inner recitation of grievances against him (and a number of other men and women). There is a stirring memory of an instance of his early courtship. There are more stirring memories of other men's attentions and courtships— some repellant, some welcome, some achieved. The whole forty-five pages are unpunctuated, almost unparagraphed. Her stream-of-consciousness—or unconsciousness, or unconscious consciousness—is interrupted by bits of song, a bell tolling the hour, a train going by in the distance, shopping lists of food, clothes, jewelry.

It is also a recapitulation of the single day that Leopold Bloom and Stephen Dedalus have spent in various parts of Dublin.

It's all packed in. A good way to unpack it is to listen to Siobhan McKenna's recording of it. That came out on a 33 rpm LP, which may be available on iTunes.

It is chiefly this section that caused *Ulysses* to be banned as obscene.

Yes I think he made them a bit firmer sucking them like that so long he made me thirsty titties he calls them I had to laugh yes this one anyhow stiff the nipple gets for the least thing Ill get him to keep that up and Ill take those eggs beaten up with marsala fatten them out for him what are all those veins and things curious the way its made 2 the same in case of twins theyre supposed to represent beauty placed up there like those statues in the museum one of them pretending to hide it with her hand are they so beautiful of course compared with what a man looks like with his two bags full and his other thing hanging down out of him or sticking up like a hatrack.

On the other hand:

I wished he was here or somebody to let myself go with and come again like that I feel all fire inside me or if I could dream it when he made me spend the 2nd time tickling me behind with his finger I was coming for about 5 minutes with my legs around him I had to hug him after O Lord I wanted to shout out all sort of things fuck or shit.

The "obscene language" is one thing that made this a pioneering work. It took a dozen years before *Ulysses* was allowed into the United States. See *United States v. One Book Called "Ulysses"* 5 F. Supp. 182 (SDNY 1933). But the more interesting pioneering is the stream-of-consciousness. As a method of storytelling in even these last forty-five pages it does the work of a novel, but it asks that the reader have very good eye-brain coordination.

Molly Bloom's stream-of-consciousness moves in cycles from idle thought to sour reflection to sexual fantasy to semisweet memory, breaking off when a noise from the sleepless mechanical world—a far-off train or a bell in a clock tower—reminds her that she's sleepless too.

The last cycle begins two pages from the very end—a bit about Bloom and his taste for her: "Ill let him do it off on me behind provided he doesnt smear all my good drawers O I suppose that cant be helped," then "a quarter after what an unearthly hour," then Molly's dreamily preparing for a visit from Bloom's young friend Stephen Dedalus whom she fancies ("whatll I wear shall I wear a white rose or those fairy cakes in Liptons I love the smell of a rich big shop at 7 ½d a lb") and then a short mental quarrel with atheists ("who was the first person in the universe before there was anybody that made it all who ah that they dont know neither do I so there you are they might as well try to stop the sun from rising tomorrow"). It is the sun that cues Molly's page-long final aria ("the sun shines for you he said the day we were lying among the rhododendrons on Howth head").

That was long ago—

> the day I got him to propose to me yes first I gave him the bit of seedcake out of my mouth yes sixteen years ago my God after that long kiss I near lost my breath yes he said I was a flower of the mountain yes so we are flowers all a woman's body yes that was one true thing he said in his life and the sun shines for you today yes

Then Molly's young years in Gibraltar where her father was stationed

> and the old castle thousands of years old yes and those handsome Moors and turbans like kings." "O and the sea the sea crimson sometimes like fire and the glorious sunsets and the figtrees in the Alameda gardens yes . . . Gibraltar as a girl where I was a Flower of the mountain yes when I put the rose in my hair like the Andalusian girls used or shall I wear a red yes and how he kissed me under the Moorish wall and I thought well as well him as another and then I asked him with my eyes to ask again yes and then he asked me would I yes to say yes my mountain flower and first I put my arms

around him yes and drew him down to me so he could feel
my breasts all perfume yes and his heart was going like mad
and yes I said yes I will Yes

Ten times yes in ten lines. Four times yes in the tenth line.
The last word Yes.

Cathexis and release. Why am I shy to write "orgasm"?
Because I'm shy to intrude such a spasmodic word into Molly's
Bloom's pure ascension.

ME ME GAB

The many and various persons in the first person.

ERE IS an excerpt from a form letter from Sarah Heckin
Redfield, director of the Heckin Foundation's fiction division. The foundation offers a $10,000 fellowship to an author
with an exemplary novel in progress.

> Dear [blank],
>
> This is to inform you that your novel-in-progress
> was not advanced to the finalist round.
>
> Fellowships applicants like to know why their
> work did not proceed to the finalist round, and
> though we do not have the time to give individual cri-
> tiques, I can share with you the problems and trends
> found in the novels in this year's semi-final round.

Before I proceed, I would like to say on behalf
of the foundation that we respect the courage and
commitment that new writers exhibited in this year's
competition. Writing fiction in the nineties is a very
difficult process. The following comments are not
designed to dishearten you.

Ninety-six percent of the manuscripts we read
were written in the first person . . .

Let me say here that in spite of Ms. Redfield's kind intentions
not to dishearten, I was disheartened, even though I was not one
of the applicants. But before I take exception, a few more words
from Ms. Redfield.

It is very common for new writers to begin with
a first-person work. All of us, myself included have
been taught to "write what you know." We know our
lives best, so that's what we tend to write about. But
where's the story? . . . My life, for example, from its
inception until now, is not a story. It's a history, as all
lives are, but it is not a story. This is not to say that
there are not moments in our own lives that we can
draw on when we write fiction, but we should not rely
on our daily existence for fiction.

Well, call me Ishmael . . .

I'm afraid that I am being unkind to Ms. Redfield. But not
unfair. Here are some notes about the variety of possibilities
beyond ME ME GAB that the first person offers.

When I was sixteen or seventeen, an old—he must have been
forty—actor came to my high school to be the entertainment for

the Friday morning assembly. Normally we had lectures on government. This actor was probably at leisure and unlikely to find parts as he was an old-fashioned elocutionary performer in the John Barrymore style—a thespian. But he changed me a good deal. He recited—performed—this Robert Browning piece.

MY LAST DUCHESS

That's my last Duchess painted on the wall,
Looking as if she were alive. I call
That piece a wonder, now: Frà Pandolf's hands
Worked busily a day, and there she stands.
Will't please you sit and look at her? I said
"Frà Pandolf" by design, for never read
Strangers like you that pictured countenance,
The depth and passion of its earnest glance,
But to myself they turned (since none puts by
The curtain I have drawn for you, but I)
And seemed as they would ask me, if they durst,
How such a glance came there; so, not the first
Are you to turn and ask thus. Sir 'twas not
Her husband's presence only, called that spot
Of joy into the Duchess' cheek: perhaps
Frà Pandolf chanced to say "Her mantle laps
Over my lady's wrist too much," or "Paint
Must never hope to reproduce the faint
Half-flush that dies along her throat": such stuff
Was courtesy, she thought, and cause enough
For calling up that spot of joy. She had
A heart—how shall I say?—too soon made glad,
Too easily impressed; she liked what'er

She looked on, and her looks went everywhere.
Sir, 'twas all one! My favor at her breast,
The drooping of the daylight in the West,
The bough of cherries some officious fool
Broke in the orchard for her, the white mule
She rode with round the terrace—all and each
Would draw from her alike the approving speech,
Or blush, at least. She thanked men,—good! but
    thanked
Somehow—I know not how—as if she ranked
My gift of a nine-hundred-years-old name
With anybody's gift. Who'd stoop to blame
This sort of trifling? Even had you skill
In speech—which I have not—to make your will
Quite clear to such an one, and say, "Just this
Or that in you disgusts me; here you miss,
Or there exceed the mark"—and if she let
Herself be lessoned so, nor plainly set
Her wits to yours, forsooth, and made excuse,
—E'en then would be some stooping; and I choose
Never to stoop. Oh sir, she smiled, no doubt,
Whene'er I passed her; but who passed without
Much the same smile? This grew; I gave commands;
Then all smiles stopped together. There she stands
As if alive. Will't please you rise? We'll meet
The company below, then. I repeat,
The Count your master's known munificence
Is ample warrant that no just pretense
Of mind for dowry will be disallowed;
Though his fair daughter's self, as I avowed
At starting, is my Object. Nay, we'll go

Together down, sir. Notice Neptune, though,
Taming a sea-horse, thought a rarity,
Which Claus of Innsbruck cast in bronze for me!

I had two reactions. One was a wonderful visceral horror at the exposure, as if of a monstrous deformity, of the duke's villainy. I had, more completely than at Saturday matinees at the Apex movie theater, suspended my disbelief.

My other reaction was an aftershock of admiration, which in my innocent confusion I bestowed entirely on the actor. I may have even thought he wrote it. My admiration was for the device of the elegant but involuntarily self-revealing speaker. That's how I took it at the time—a villain who lets it slip because, although a man of high culture, he is obtuse to good or evil.

The actor also performed some Edgar Allan Poe stories—which I lapped up too. I don't know if I knew the difference in texture—when you are awakened like that, you are indiscriminate but I think not guilty by reason of enthusiasm.

The opening paragraph of "The Cask of Amontillado":

The thousand injuries of Fortunato I had borne as I best could; but when he ventured upon insult, I vowed revenge. You, who so well know the nature of my soul, will not suppose, however, that I gave utterance to a threat. *At length* I would be avenged.

From "The Black Cat":

The cat followed me down the steep stairs, and, nearly throwing me headlong, exasperated me to madness. Uplifting an axe, and forgetting in my wrath the childish dread which had hitherto stayed my hand, I aimed a blow at the animal, which, of course, would have proved instantly fatal had it descended as I wished. But this blow was arrested by the hand of my wife. Goaded by the interference into a rage more than demoniacal, I withdrew my arm from her grasp and buried the axe in her brain. She fell dead upon the spot without a groan.

The hideous murder accomplished, I set myself forthwith, and with entire deliberation, to the task of concealing the body . . .

And so to the gory end:

Of my own thoughts it is folly to speak. Swooning, I staggered to the opposite wall. For one instant the party upon the stairs remained motionless, through extremity of terror and of awe. In the next, a dozen stout arms were toiling at the wall. It fell bodily. The corpse, already greatly decayed and clotted with gore, stood erect before the eyes of the spectators. Upon its head, with red extended mouth and solitary eye of fire, sat the hideous beast whose craft had seduced me into murder, and whose informing voice had consigned me to the hangman. I had walled the monster up within the tomb.

Some years later I read *The Good Soldier* by Ford Madox Ford—so I did have another exposure to the device of the defective narrator—but the primal experience was "My Last Duchess." And it came back to me when I started to write—not the early stuff, but the second cycle. I had written a novel while in law school. It is my impression, contrary to Ms. Heckin Redfield's, that early novels that attempt autobiography are usually in the third person.

The third person is easier to rig out in wished-for virtues, acts, and above all, luminous feelings and witty sayings. That first novel was not so much fiction as it was false.

When I took a chapter from it and rewrote it, I achieved two things. I'd chewed the raw material of peacetime army life and ruminated, so it was now halfway to fiction. Putting it in the first person gave me freedom from autobiographical self-justification, freedom to perform. It was impersonal impersonation. I was also able to *build a character*, the way an actor does. It was freedom and it was discipline. The device itself made me write fiction that was much truer to the mixture of goodwill and arrogance, of what had been decent in my twenty-year-old self and what had been tainted. But more important, this device suggested the need for more material, and the new material increased my knowledge and skill at handling the device and its special leverages and limitations.

I wrote a cycle of stories using this same device; a well-educated young man with a set of received ideas but also with a blind spot tells a story about himself, involuntarily on himself.

A footnote. The title of the cycle is *Testimony and Demeanor.* This is a phrase that a judge often uses in instructing a jury— something like this—"Ladies and Gentlemen of the jury—you may decide what weight to give the evidence offered by a witness by evaluating *the testimony and demeanor* of the witness."

The third story in the cycle gave me a lot of trouble. I had a rough draft of a melodrama, which I turned into a more interesting novella in the first person—closer to something in the zone of okay fiction but still not quite right. The narrator was too much of a regular guy. At that time a young writer arrived in Iowa City who'd gone to Yale, who was well born, in fact half FFV, half New York WASP, but most of all beautifully dressed. It was the first time I'd seen a blue shirt with a white collar—the second time a wasp-waisted tweed jacket with double vents. I borrowed his clothes for my narrator. Sometimes an actor who's been uninspired finally gets it when he gets his costume on. After three months of rewriting, I thought he was ready to go on.

Here's how I found the cycle was over. I got a very French idea. At least too French for me. I started writing a story told by an unreliable narrator who gets to the blank page *before the author.* He wrote, "Before that perverse and nasty writer gets here, let me tell you: I am not as bad or dumb as he's going to make me out. Please—when he says 'I,' it's not me."

And a bit later: "He's gone out for a coffee. I just have time to tell you—I have never whined like that in my life."

So there is the first-person narrator who is in some way defective—obtuse, unreliable, and so on—but whose defect can be used to compress and crystallize a story. There is a slightly different category of first-person narrator—type 1B—and that is the reliable-but-limited-by-circumstance narrator. It's the truth, it's voluntary, but it's just one point of view. The best examples I can think of are the two trilogies by Joyce Cary, a writer whose star I'd like to see rise again. The more colorful trilogy, and the one I'd recommend first (but not necessarily more highly), is *Herself Surprised, To Be A Pilgrim,* and *The Horse's Mouth.*

Herself Surprised is narrated by Sara Monday, who is sometimes in love or at least in bed with the painter Gulley Jimson, but who is married to Chester Nimmo, a more pious, productive, and respected member of society but, as we learn from his narration in volume 3, a man with a heart as passionate as Sara's or Gulley Jimson's. It is of course Gulley Jimson who narrates Volume 2, *The Horse's Mouth.* (That novel was turned into a very good movie, which won't spoil your enjoyment of the book, as it is distinct from it.)

The overall effect of the three-way split in first person narration is that the whole is greater than the sum of the parts. While you are listening to Sara you are in sympathy with her—and in *The Horse's Mouth* you sympathize with Gulley Jimson and in *To Be a Pilgrim* with Chester Nimmo. There is an old rule of writing from the days of the slick magazines (as opposed to the pulps): If you want to gain sympathy for your protagonist, show him or her trying to do something. Readers, who are the most benign people in the world, will root for a character making an effort, even beyond the limits of their own moral code—for example, if we read a step by step account of someone trying to get into a bank vault, we want to see him succeed. Joyce Cary takes his sympathy to a grand scale—his three characters are *trying to lead their lives*—and then he leans them against each other like the poles of a teepee.

TYPE 2

The double first person: the "I" as "I was" and the "I" as "I now am." Or the innocent "I" and the knowledgeable "I."

An example of narration in which these two "I's" operate in alternation is George Orwell's "Such, Such Were the Joys."

> Soon after I arrived at St. Cyprian's (not immediately, but after a week or two, just when I seemed to be settling into the routine of school life), I began wetting my bed. I was now aged eight, so that this was reversion to a habit which I must have grown out of at least four years earlier.

Here the alternation of reliving—the then-"I"—with an adult view—the now-"I" is rapid: "Nowadays" to "In those days."

> Nowadays, I believe, bed-wetting in such circumstances is taken for granted. It is a normal reaction in children who

have been removed from their homes to a strange place. In those days, however, it was looked on as a disgusting crime which the child committed on purpose and for which the proper cure was a beating. . . .

After the second or third offence I was warned that I should be beaten next time, but I received the warning in a curiously roundabout way. One afternoon, as we were filing out from tea, Mrs. Wilkes, the Headmaster's wife, was sitting at the head of one of the tables, chatting with a lady of whom I knew nothing. . . . She was an intimidating, masculine-looking person wearing a riding-habit.

"Here is a little boy," said Flip, [Mrs. Wilke's nickname], "who wets his bed every night. Do you know what I am going to do if you wet your bed again?" she added, turning to me. "I am going to get the Sixth Form to beat you."

. . . And here there occurred one of those wild, almost lunatic misunderstanding which are part of the daily experience of childhood. I mis-heard the phrase "the Sixth Form" as "Mrs. Form." It was an improbable name, but a child has no judgment in such matters.

And so the memoir continues—incident after incident relived in the voice of a child—bed-wetting, Latin class, the turd in the school swimming pool, the sophisticated English snobbisms of the very young boys—and each incident then commented on and analyzed by the fully grown George Orwell who had developed his adult "I" to such a careful and powerful honesty in his essays that he came to be known, rightly, as the conscience of his age. This essayistic "I" that Orwell developed is a marvel—it is a levelheaded "I," the essence of good common sense, the result one assumes of a scrupulous self-examination. I think that is true—but without contradicting it, or in any way calling it untruthful, I have also come to think that Orwell's "I" is a work of art.

ORWELL'S REAL NAME is Eric Blair—he preferred George Orwell because Eric Blair was too likely to have gone to Eton, too unlikely a name to speak up from the ranks on their *behalf as one of them*, the name of an "I" difficult to believe was truly down and out in Paris or London.

Here is a paragraph (italics added) from Orwell's book *Homage to Catalonia*; Orwell was sent to Barcelona to report on the Spanish Civil War.

> Down the Ramblas, the wide central artery of the town where crowds of people streamed constantly to and fro, the loudspeakers were bellowing revolutionary songs all day and far into the night. And it was the aspect of the crowds that was the queerest thing of all. In outward appearance it was a town in which the wealthy classes had practically ceased to exist. Except for a small number of women and foreigners there were no "well dressed" people at all. Practically everyone wore rough working-class clothes or blue overalls or some variant of the militia uniform. All this was queer and moving. *There was much in it that I did not understand, in some ways I did not even like it, but I recognized it immediately as a state of affairs worth fighting for.*

I now value that last sentence for its beauty as much as for its truth. I feel the swoon that Orwell's "I" felt when at last he met something he could fall in love with—as much that as a resolve to make the world a better place, free from the injuries of class. Both true.

I'm recommending and citing all this Orwell as part of a consideration of first-person narration because I think Orwell has forged an "I" out of art as well as life. The Orwell "I," the reliable, narrator is not innate, not given. But just because it is chosen, just because it is willed (and in Orwell's case wonderfully expanded and realized), it does not follow that it doesn't see truly, or that it is itself untrue. That it is a literary act is not a subtraction. It is an addition that we can admire—possibly imitate. Its effect on some readers is that the "I" is intimate and universal, that there is such a sensory transfusion of experience and reflection that the reader receives both an immediate and a mediated English boarding school or a state of affairs in Barcelona worth fighting for. (Not a rhetorical phrase: Orwell joined the militia, fought, and was shot through the throat—and survived to see the Loyalists beaten by Fascists and betrayed by the Comintern.)

The double I.

The then-now narrator in Marcel Proust's *Remembrance of Things Past* is a then-"I" of aspiration and a now-"I" of salvation. Proust's salvation is the recapturing of the then by the now—the past retasted in a sacrament. It is an artistic and personal (as opposed to Orwell's political and common) fulfillment. It is also a way of having your petite madeleine and eating it too. It is the answer to the common sigh, "If only I knew then what I know now."

Here is the skeleton of a sample paragraph. Setting: a hotel room at Balbec. Two adolescents. "I found Albertine in bed" . . . "I bent over Albertine to kiss her. 'Stop it or I'll ring the bell!' cried Albertine" . . . "Albertine pulled the bell with all her might." But the passage has gone on for almost six hundred words. It is filled with parenthetical reflections that belong more to the now "I" than to a fumbling adolescent trying to kiss a young girl in bed with a cold.

A moment of disappointment and embarrassment that makes one numb but rediscovered by the now-"I," the then-"I's" numbness is transformed through Marcel's later absorption of all the arts of Europe, into an "I" who is forever panting.

TYPE 3

A perplexity of first-person narration: The illogically isolated "I" of then.

How can a narrator talk as if she doesn't know what's going to happen next when she's telling the story after it's over? How can he talk to us in a voice that is untransformed by the transformations he has already undergone?

David Copperfield says, "Whether I shall turn out to be the hero of my own life or whether that station will be held by anybody else, these pages must show."

Should we wait with bated breath?

Or is it a joke?

A CLEAR EXAMPLE of the then-I/now-I is in *The Autobiography of Malcolm X* as told to Alex Haley. This is an amazing and valuable book, but for our purposes I'd like to note only that although Malcolm X accepts Allah and is horrified by his earlier life of vice and crime, when he describes it there is a relived exuberance and even swagger.

> He motioned for me to sniff some. The only word to describe it was a *timelessness*.
>
> As I hung up, I spotted two lean, tough-looking *paisanos* gazing in at me cooped up in the booth.

And I had no gun. A cigarette case was the only thing in my pocket. I started easing my hand down into my pockets, to try bluffing . . .

I was still shaking when I got to the apartment of my friend, Sammy the Pimp . . . Sammy and I sniffed some of his cocaine.

The pimping was so poor, Sammy had gone on the job with me. We had selected one of those situations considered "impossible." But wherever people think that, guards will unconsciously grow gradually more relaxed, until sometimes those can be the easiest jobs of all.

*   *   *

The spotlight was working mostly just us. . . .

Some of the men in the band applauded. And even Duke Ellington half raised up from his piano stool and bowed.

And I was being pounded on the back . . . when I caught this fine blonde's eyes. This one I'd never seen among the white girls who came to the Roseland black dances. She was eyeing me levelly . . .

About five blocks down she had a low convertible . . . she knew where she was going . . . She pulled off into a side road, and then off that into a deserted lane. And turned off everything but the radio.

And then conversion and repentance:

I have never previously told anyone my sordid past in detail. I haven't done it now to sound as though I might be proud of how bad, how evil, I was . . .

. . . [T]he full story is the best way that I know to have

it seen and understood that I had sunk to the very bottom of the American white man's society when—soon now, in prison—I found Allah and the religion of Islam and it completely transformed my life."

The *full* story means *reliving* it. And confessions are more valuable when they show that Saint Augustine's or Malcolm X's early days were understandably pleasurable.

Nancy Reagan's "Just say no" isn't as good as Nancy my cousin saying, "Cocaine is wonderful—I just wish I could do it without turning myself into the girl who skipped Mom's funeral. Not to mention the last year of her life."

I used to explain away this illogicality, the perplexity of the isolated young "I" by citing "Flowers for Algernon," a science-fiction short story that came out in 1959. (It was subsequently turned into a novel—not as good). A retarded man keeps a diary of his being tested as a guinea pig with an intelligence-enhancing drug.

March Report:
I told Dr. Strauss and perfesser Nemur I can't rite good but he says it dont matter he says I shud rite just like I talk.

June Report
12. Our relationship is becoming increasingly strained. I resent Nemur's constant references to me as a laboratory specimen.

The narrator learns enough science to prove that the way Nemur has put the drug together will have a rebound effect in another three months. The rest of the diary entries go downhill: "November 21—I did a dumb thing today I forgot I wasnt in [the] class at the adult center any more like I use to be."

It's pathos, but in its short-story form it had an old-fashioned whiz-bang sci-fi effect—and it was the purest diary form in which every entry was sealed off from every other. I thought that perhaps every first-person narrative has a ghost of a diary form hovering nearby and that readers, sensing this, summon the diary form, feel it as a phantom limb. I don't disavow this as an explanation of the reader response. But we could also put the phantom form in the author's psyche. It's all still there. Proust says so. Malcolm X says so. Not just the event but the experience. You can call up your past in pure diary form, or in light of the repentance, or in alternation or mixing of the two. The perplexity is a problem only if you believe that the self is an integer, rather than also being a collection of all one's days stored in our souls both *seriatim et simulator,* both as shish kebab and as stew.

TYPE 4

The swelling "I," I am all . . .

> Walt Whitman am I, a Kosmos, of mighty Manhat-
> tan the son . . .
> Through me the afflatus surging and surging—
> through me the current and index.

But he's generous with his totality.

> "All I mark as my own you shall offset it with your own
> Else it were time lost listening to me."

A final "I" into "we." Which you'll recognize. And you'll

remember that the narrator is a sideline character but one who has the leverage to lift the whole novel into the air.

> Most of the big shore places were closed now and there were hardly any lights except the shadowy, moving glow of a ferryboat across the Sound. And as the moon rose higher the inessential houses began to melt away until gradually I became aware of the old island here that flowered once for Dutch sailors' eyes—a fresh, green breast of the New World. Its vanished trees, the trees that had made way for Gatsby's house, had once pandered in whispers to the last and greatest of all human dreams; for a transitory enchanted moment man must have held his breath in the presence of this continent . . .
>
> And as I sat there brooding on the old, unknown world, I thought of Gatsby's wonder when he first picked out the green light at the end of Daisy's dock. He had come a long way to this blue lawn, and his dream must have seemed so close that he could hardly fail to grasp it. He did not know that it was already behind him, somewhere back in that vast obscurity beyond the city, where the dark fields of the republic rolled on under the night.
>
> Gatsby believed in the green light, the orgastic future that year by year recedes before us. It eluded me then, but that's no matter—tomorrow we will run faster, stretch out our arms farther . . . And one fine morning—
>
> So we beat on, boats against the current, borne back ceaselessly into the past.

In these final chords the language dilates from particular to general, from narrative to vision, to anthem and antianthem; and the narrator dilates from "I" to "us."

The first-person defective narrator; limited narrator; narrator as ghost of the past and future, young and old, innocent and knowledgeable; the common-conscience narrator; the narrator alive again in the past, the narrator as diarist and diary; the narrator as you, the narrator as we—this list of first-person possibilities is preliminary, not inclusive. Russell Banks, having heard my catalog, told me that it's good but that there is still more to the "I." When I read his novel *Rule of the Bone*, I tipped my hat.

MEANWHILE BACK AT THE RANCH

Polyphony in prose—is it possible? An examination of attempts to add a simultaneous other voice to a narrative. An analogy is to the "sympathetic strings" of a viola da gamba. The sympathetic strings, while not bowed, resonate to create an accompaniment.

James Salter, Vladimir Nabokov, Gustave Flaubert, and Anton Chekhov come very, very close.

IN GENERAL, people who write prose fiction don't set themselves formal problems—at least there's not a list of acknowledged challenges like squaring the circle or finding the unified field theory. And there aren't even lots of neat forms, like fugues or sonnets or villanelles.

The only *definition* of a novel that I remember is an old joke: a novel is a long piece of prose that has something wrong with it.

There are *content* challenges. Lots of content challenges. Write about this region, about that class. The challenge I remember most clearly is that every so often some civic-minded readers wish that novelists would concern themselves with national life, with politics, with something bigger than intimate lives. But, in America at least, this challenge doesn't have many takers. *All the King's Men*, *The Last Hurrah*, and a few others. I don't think there's a really good novel set in Washington. *Democracy* by Henry Brooks Adams is too ill tempered to be more than a satirical tirade, a shadow play of an essay. Maybe this lack comes about because novels depend on a character's free will, and by the time a politician gets to Washington, free will is severely circumscribed. The choice part of free will is already spent, and what's left of will, however right and good, is just the effort.

There are some technical problems that fiction writers cope with—point-of-view shifts, first-person narrators and their blind spots—but these don't interest the general reader as much as they do the writer, and most of these problems aren't all that hard anyway, not compared to things like people, place, tone, or plot, which are big, even amorphous, but specific to each particular story.

However, from time to time one problem does pop up that may be the equivalent of a formal problem and may be, if not the Holy Grail, a neat challenge.

In the play *Amadeus* someone asks Mozart why he's so fond of opera. The answer is duets, trios, sextets. And what's so good about them? Mozart says, as I recall, that in a story or in a play only one person can speak at one time, but when people sing, the audience can hear and understand two, three, six voices at once—each voice with its own tune, its own emotion.

I was knocked out. I thought, Gee, you sure can't do that on the printed page.

Later on I thought that you might get a little bit of simultaneity in a play. You can have one actor speak, and you can have another actor react.

"My dear," X says to Y, "I love you!" *while* Y looks terribly pained even as X speaks.

Y then says, "Oh, how sad!" and X's face is already a mask of grief. Y goes on to say, "For I must tell you that my heart is pledged to another!"

Meanwhile Z, lurking behind a bush, turns to the audience revealing a face so radiant with hope that Z doesn't even have to step on Y's line by uttering a single word, let alone the complete sentence "Oh joy! Could Y mean me?"

It's not Mozart; it's not Don Giovanni, Donna Elvira, Donna Anna, Don Ottavio, and Leporello all going at it together. But still I saw that a play could be more richly simultaneous than reading one word after another in a straight time line.

Then I remembered an effort from years ago. It was at the Iowa Writers' Workshop. A very smart fellow apprentice brought into one workshop a story written in three different colors. Green—the thoughts of a man in a jealous frenzy. Black—the medieval bestiary he was reading at that very moment. Red— while at the same time the man's wife is rapturously embracing her lover. In the author's attempt to make all three colors happen at once, he had cut up each sentence into fragments so that you read a little green, a bit of black, some red and so forth. The effect of a single sentence was something like this: "HE GROUND HIS / *unicorns and gryphons* / biting and kissing and biting / TEETH AND GRIPPED / *rampant on a field of azure* / her calves and the hollow behind her knee / WITH HIS RIGHT HAND THE GROOVED ARMREST OF HIS CHAIR."

For a half page we were spellbound, or at least trying hard to be spellbound, but by the end of the page, everyone got a terrible headache. At least there was that simultaneity: fifteen people

with the same headache. Meanwhile, back at the ranch, everyone took two aspirin.

Some years later I read *Light Years* by James Salter, a novel
that I loved, although a friend of mine summed it up as "luminously depressing." In any case I recognized an attempt at
simultaneity, this time in more capable hands, a less raw experiment. In this short paragraph a wife is on her way home from
her lover's house:

> Her car was parked outside. It was afternoon, winter, the
> trees were bare. Her children were in class, writing in large
> letters, making silver and green maps of the states.
>
> Viri [her husband] came home in the darkness, head-
> lights blazing his approach, illuminating the trees . . .
>
> The door closed behind him. He came in from the eve-
> ning air, cool and whitened, as if from the sea.
>
> "Hello, Viri," she said.
>
> A fire was burning. His children were laying out forks.

Wife. Car. Afternoon. Trees. Her children in school.
Husband. Car. Night. Trees. His children laying out forks.
We have the same quick shift of point of view as in the green,
black, and red, and it is a trio, but it works better because there
are two almost identical visual fields, with a few notes the same
(car, trees, children) and a few notes different (afternoon/eve-
ning; their children writing large letters / their children laying
out forks).

And of course our dramatic intelligence is appreciating the
lies that bind.

It was after I read *Light Years* that I came back to *Madame
Bovary* and found what is probably the most influential sample of
this sort of back-and-forth near simultaneity. It is in the scene of

Rodolphe's first success with Madame Bovary, which takes place at the agricultural fair at Yonville.

The fair starts with Flaubert at his satirical best—a handful of Yonvillian characters puffing themselves up for the celebration, filled with the false sentiment and false consciousness that Flaubert despised—and loved to despise. The animal side of the fair, however, brings out an exuberance in Flaubert that makes him a master painter of large scenes. He gives us the whole fairground in tableau—the pigs, sheep, calves, cows, a magnificent bull, stallions, mares, foals. All the colors of the sky, the animals and the earth, and all the smells and sounds.

Flaubert is a wonderful knot: he loves the sensual and is in a rage at the misuse of the sensual.

The officials are farcical. There is a case of mistaken identity of the honored visitor, the one-gun salute goes off too soon, the "[P]resent arms!" of the guard sounds like a copper pot bouncing down the stairs, and the guest official begins an inflated speech.

The visiting subprefect says—and here you must imagine a pathetic man orating like Charles de Gaulle:

> "Messieurs: To the monarch, gentlemen, our sovereign, to that beloved king to whom no branch of public or private prosperity is a matter of indifference . . .

In the shadow inside the second-floor window, Rodolphe murmurs to Madame Bovary,

> "[But happiness] comes one day . . . one day suddenly, when one is despairing of it . . . it glitters, it flashes, yet one still doubts, one does not dare to believe in it, one is dazzled as if one came out of the darkness into light." And as he ended

Rodolphe suited the action to the word, he passed his hand over his face like a man seized with giddiness. Then he let his hand fall on Emma's. She withdrew her hand.

The orator having saluted the king, salutes the farmer, the larger livestock, and still has a flourish for the hen.

"Who has not frequently reflected on all the momentous things that we extract from that modest animal, ornament of our barnyards, who furnishes us simultaneously with a down pillow for our heads, its succulent flesh for our table, and eggs?"

Rodolphe had drawn nearer to Emma and said to her in a low voice, speaking rapidly,

"Does not this conspiracy of the world revolt you? The purest sympathies are persecuted, slandered; and if at last two poor souls do meet, it's all organized so that they cannot join together."

Another orator goes on about primitive man eating acorns in the forest. Rodolphe gets to dreams, presentiments, animal magnetism. The orator to weaving, to the planted field, the vine. Rodolphe goes from animal magnetism to affinities. The orator does Cincinnatus at his plow, the Chinese emperor inaugurating the new year at the spring planting. Rodolphe explains that this irresistible attraction may be caused by their having known each other in past lives. He takes her hand. She does not take it away.

So we have two comic arenas—political bullshit below and private bullshit above. Flaubert is savage and disdainful in his presentation of the duet of false notes.

But tucked into this counterpoint of bullshit—which by the way is having its effect on both Madame Bovary and on the crowd—tucked into a little niche there is a sweet internal song of Emma Bovary's (who once daydreamed about a waltz partner and then had a deep but unconsummated crush on young Leon):

> She saw in [Rodolphe's] eyes the small gold lines radiating from his black pupils—she even smelled the odor of his pomade with which he slicked his hair. Then a softness came over her—she remembered the viscount who had waltzed with her at Vaubyessard whose beard had given off this odor of vanilla and lemon, and mechanically she half closed her eyes to breathe it in. But in making this movement, as she leaned back in her chair, she saw in the distance on the horizon the old stagecoach "The Swallow" which was coming down the hill from Leux, trailing after it a long plume of dust. It was in this yellow carriage that Leon had so often come back to her, and by that very road over there that he had left forever. She thought she saw his face across the square at his window and then everything became confused. Clouds passed. It seemed to her that she was turning in the waltz under the flame of the chandeliers on the arm of the viscount, and that Leon was not far off, that he was coming, and yet all the while she was aware of the scent of Rodolphe's head by her side. The sweetness of this present sensation pierced her old desires, and they were blown, like grains of sand by a wind, into the subtle movement that was spreading over her soul.

Rodolphe completes his seduction after a few more days. He is heavy-handedly skillful and is quite pleased with himself at first. And then he becomes fearful of what he has aroused. That's an old—though usually interesting—story.

But it isn't Rodolphe as cad and master hypnotist who is the point of interest. It is Madame Bovary as self-hypnotist. And it is the *little* simultaneity of the viscount, the waltz, the chandeliers—and sweet young Leon, and the gold-flecked eyes and brilliantined hair of Rodolphe—it is that little inward spiral of accumulated imaginative desire—conveyed by sound, sight, *and* smell—that is the true centerpiece of the loud outdoor agricultural fair at Yonville with its broader counterpoints.

That little spiral has another simultaneity. The passage is an implicitly harsh judgment on Emma Bovary, for her synthetic easy imagination, but Flaubert enters that imagination with a lot of sympathy. Along with her imperfect sense of things, Flaubert gives her vivid senses—and I don't think I'm imagining the undertone of his love for her, even as he sends her on her way from foolishness to foolishness to despair.

Another example of *how* prose writers attempt simultaneity, and then I'll say why. In this passage from *Speak, Memory*, Nabokov gives a sketch of his father—a man who was ultimately killed in exile by a right-wing émigré. This scene is also largely visual, and for most of it, the tone is that of an amused, distant raconteur. But just near the end, Nabokov shifts the tone—in midair to overlay his anecdote with something more passionate.

> The old and the new, the liberal touch and the patriarchal one, fatal poverty and fatalistic wealth got fantastically interwoven in that strange first decade of our century. Several times during a summer it might happen that in the middle of luncheon, in the bright, many-windowed, walnut-paneled dining room on the first floor of our Vyra manor, Aleksey, the butler, with an unhappy expression on his face, would bend over and inform my father in a low voice (especially low if we had company) that a group of villagers wanted to

see the *barin* outside. Briskly my father would remove his napkin from his lap and ask my mother to excuse him. One of the windows at the west end of the dining room gave upon a portion of the drive near the main entrance. One could see the top of the honeysuckle bushes opposite the porch. From that direction the courteous buzz of a peasant welcome would reach us as the invisible group greeted my invisible father. The ensuing parley, conducted in ordinary tones, would not be heard, as the windows underneath which it took place were closed to keep out the heat. It presumably had to do with a plea for his mediation in some local feud, or with some special subsidy, or with the permission to harvest some bit of our land or cut down a coveted clump of our trees. If, as unusually happened, the request was at once granted, there would be again that buzz, and then, in token of gratitude, the good *barin* would be put through the national ordeal of being rocked and tossed and securely caught by a score or so of strong arms.

In the dining room, my brother and I would be told to go on with our food. My mother, a tidbit between finger and thumb, would glance under the table to see if her nervous and gruff dachshund was there. *"Un jour ils vont le laisser tomber,"* would come from Mlle Golay, a primly pessimistic old lady who had been my mother's governess and still dwelt with us (on awful terms with our own governesses). From my place at table I would suddenly see through one of the west windows a marvelous case of levitation. There, for an instant, the figure of my father in his wind-rippled white summer suit would be displayed, gloriously sprawling in midair, his limbs in a curiously casual attitude, his handsome, imperturbable features turned to the sky. Thrice, to the mighty heave-ho of his invisible tossers, he would fly up in this fashion, and the second time he would go higher than the first and then there he would be, on his last and loftiest flight, reclining, as if for good, against the cobalt blue of the summer noon like one of those paradisiac personages who comfortably soar, with such a wealth of folds in their garments, on the vaulted ceiling of a church while below, one by one, the wax tapers in mortal hands light up to make a swarm of minute flames in the mist of incense, and the priest chants of eternal repose, and funeral lilies conceal the face of whoever lies there, among the swimming lights, in the open coffin.

It's hard to find the exact point at which the seignorial reminiscence turns into a requiem. Is it "and then there he would be, on his last and loftiest flight, reclining, as if for good, against the cobalt blue of the summer noon"?

Not yet, not completely—because we still get a bit of the raconteur in "like one of those paradisiac personages who comfortably soar, with such a wealth of folds in their garments."

The sensual part of the reader's brain is still lit by "the cobalt blue of the summer noon" while the grammatical brain is alerting itself to the aptness of the simile: "like one of those paradisiac personages."

But the simile is extended and extended until it finally engulfs the anecdote: "while below, one by one, the wax tapers in mortal hands light up . . . and the priest chants of eternal repose, and funeral lilies conceal the face of whoever lies there, among the swimming lights, in the open coffin."

The prose has a highly enameled texture, both the playful and the passionate parts, but the device itself is structurally neat and strong.

It is like a scarf joint.

If you want to join two pieces of wood—to make one piece of wood out of two that are the same size—you can't just put the butt ends against each other and toenail them together. They'll wobble apart. What you do is shave each end in a long gradual diagonal. Then you fit thin to thick and thick to thin, with glue and a few tiny flathead screws, sunk flush. And you have one piece, almost as good as if it grew by nature instead of by artful composition.

It seems simple, once you've learned, but it is a very ingenious, useful device and an elegant invention.

As Nabokov's two tones overlap, thick to thin, thin to thick, there is a duet—the thin part of his passion at first as faint as the sound of someone rubbing the rim of a wineglass with a wet finger, and then it sounds larger and larger, a grief simultaneous with the cobalt blue of a summer noon.

But why attempt this simultaneity?

In *Slaughterhouse-Five* Kurt Vonnegut describes books on the planet Tralfamadore, where civilization is better than on Earth. Each book is a dot. You read it by putting it on your forehead. In my memory, I imagined it as going on the tip of your tongue. I was mixing up a microchip with a communion wafer.

The ultimate dream in an Evelyn Wood speed-reading course.

Also the ultimate dream, I think, of a novelist. What Vonnegut was getting at is that a novelist's first notion of a novel is a dot—a zap that is not a concept, not a story; in fact it first exists without language.

During the long process of writing a novel, the dot is always there, a star of wonder, westward leading, still proceeding, guiding the three kings over moor and mountain. And one of the things the novelist hopes for is that—after the reader is through the long process of reading—the reader is left with a dot zap. The novelist might also hope for a reader with total recall of every scene, every figure of speech, every mot juste—but I think that's secondary to the dot-zap wish.

How would you like a lover to remember your love affair? How would you like to remember it? Total recall of every word, every gesture, arranged in chronological order? Or a dot zap?

I may have gone too far; maybe the question isn't as rhetorical as I first thought. I suppose some might say it's both: all the moors and mountains all over again one by one *and* the star of wonder, the whole thing at once.

But the dot zap *is* one of the effects we wish for; there is a deep urge to encapsulate a person, a year, a city, a novel *not into an abstraction* but into a *chord* of simultaneous sensations. All that's on a large scale. And the dot-zap effect could be conceived by a novelist *before*—and achieved by a reader *after*—a completely linear narration. The foreshortening and overlapping needn't exist in the words on paper.

So there's still the question—why would a prose fiction writer want simultaneity in a short passage? It's not because simultaneity exists as a sort of acknowledged technical feat, as does, for example, the triple somersault for a trapeze artist.

There are reasons that arise from the nature of story writing. One of these reasons is that prose fiction has a surface texture that is often at odds with its ultimate goal. A story masquerades as sensible prose when poetic ecstasy is what it hopes for; it presents a visible world when its real goal is to conjure invisible forces; it pretends to be a chronicle, to subordinate itself to time, when its real goal is to create moments that are so compressed and crystallized that they arrest time, that they partake of God's time, in which everything happens at once.

So as a story writer you're often doing two things at once, each of which is necessary but each of which tends to negate the other.

An example of this doubleness is physical action, a staple of storytelling. The problem with physical action is this: if a character is drowning or having a tooth drilled or making love, that character, under the stress of panic or pain or ecstasy, tends to become like *anyone.* Anyone at all drowning, wincing, embracing. This is a problem because the point of a good story isn't just to create whizbang action with a crash dummy. The point is to use the action, the stress of action, to crack the shell of a character, of a character's factual life, so that the individual flavor of the psyche is released.

So willy-nilly, you're facing the problem of finding the details, the tone, the words that will sing both songs at once.

Sometimes the solution is displacement activity—a piece of action that seems logically, even dramatically irrelevant.

Displacement activity is a term from natural history, subsection, animal behavior. The concept came from an observation of a male Siamese fighting fish. The observer knew that a Siamese fighting fish would attack and drive out of his territory any smaller fighting fish. He would, however, flee from another fighting fish bigger than he. The observer put a mirror in the tank. The fighting fish charged the reflection only to discover that it was exactly the same size as himself! He floated there in midwater for a bit, caught midway between his impulse to fight and his impulse to flee. Then this male fighting fish began, quite vigorously, to build a nest.

The observer was puzzled. The male fighting fish is indeed the nest builder of the family, it is programmed to build a nest when stimulated by the female. But why now? The observer concluded that so much nervous tension had built up, both the nervous energy to fight and the energy to flee *and* the torque of wanting to do both at once, that the poor fish had to do *something*, so it short-circuited two of his instinctive responses and set off a third.

People do something like this, and fiction writers can use this behavioral tendency to write a scene that is apparently a sidebar to the story but in which the writer can let us feel the pincers of a character's predicament.

In Chekhov's "The Lady with the Dog," very near the end, the hero, Dmitri Gurov, is on his way to meet his lover, Anna Sergeyevna. They are both otherwise married. Gurov was once a heartless rake, but now, in late middle age, he finds himself doomed to an adulterous, impossible, but deep and true love. Here is the sidebar scene:

> Once he was going to see her . . . on a winter morning (the messenger had come the evening before when he was out). With him walked his daughter, whom he wanted to take to school: it was on the way. Snow was falling in big wet flakes.
>
> "It's three degrees above freezing-point, and yet it is snowing," said Gurov to his daughter. The thaw is only on the surface of the earth; there is quite a different temperature at a greater height in the atmosphere."
>
> "And why are there no thunderstorms in winter, father?"
>
> He explained that, too. He talked, thinking all the while that he was going to see her, and no living soul knew of it, and probably never would know.

The story then goes into a lovely internal aria in Gurov's mind and finally the agonizing sad-sweet lovers' meeting, as rich as the last duet in the opera of *Eugene Onegin*.

But it is the little father-daughter scene that I love most.

There's a neat, slick way of reading it: Aha, two different temperature zones—a symbol of Gurov's double life. But Gurov could have noticed the snowflakes and temperature all by himself.

I like the several things made implicit by the daughter. She is old enough to understand what Gurov is explaining in his slightly stiff and pedantic way—an awkwardness that comes over this roué only when he feels deeply (otherwise he's an old smoothie). She is still young enough to listen patiently and affectionately to her papa—she even asks for more: "And why are there no thunderstorms in winter, father?"

She is also what makes his love for Anna Sergeyevna so difficult. Gurov's wife has been presented as a social-climbing witch, a figure of satire; she is a legal-social impediment to his love, not an emotional one. Chekhov needed the daughter's voice to make a duet, to sing her own little theme and to evoke a notion of Gurov's other emotional allegiance not as an argument or rebuke but as part of Gurov's whole life as it becomes for the first time rich with love and crisis simultaneously.

You might ask, whose displacement activity am I talking about here—Gurov's or Chekhov's? I think both; I'd guess that Chekhov was so immersed in acting the part that he felt Gurov's need to displace and that Chekhov the dramatist had a sense of rhythm that gave him an awareness that the story needed to displace.

These various ways of including more than one line in a given fictional moment—whether by swift juxtaposition as in Salter's afternoon-evening passage in *Light Years*, or by a scarf joint of overlapping tones as in the Nabokov passage about his father, or by the introduction of displacement activity that releases two impulses by way of a third as in the Chekhov, or by any number of these techniques—all have something in common. I think it is an urge to charge a moment, to saturate it so intensely that it not only serves a dramatic purpose but also serves as an exemplar of how full a moment can be. It doesn't have to be sweet, just confluent.

A friend of mine quoted to me the epigraph from *The Solid Mandala* by Patrick White. Patrick White got it from Paul Éluard. I don't know whether it is desperate or hopeful, but I think it has the essence of why writers attempt simultaneity: "There is another world, but it is in this one."

SO ALERT A LANGUAGE

An examination of passages of formal high diction and of vernacular, and of some passages which mix the two to good effect.

DON'T RIGHTLY know what words to use for the categories of vocabulary I've been thinking about. *High* and *low*? Perhaps. Perhaps *lofty* for "high," though *lofty* can have an undertow of doubt.

I remember a conversation with a law professor. I was admiring the thought and, even more, the style of another law professor, John Dawson, one of the grand old men of law. Professor Jaffe heard me out and then said, "John is very . . . lofty." I felt an undertow; I thought Professor Jaffe might be thinking, I'm more down-to-earth. Or perhaps he did mean *lofty* as John Milton used it: "Who would not sing for Lycidas? he knew / Himself to sing and build the lofty rhyme."

Professor Dawson taught a course on the history of law.

Professor Jaffe taught administrative law.

When listening to Professor Dawson, I heard the echoes of centuries.

When listening to Professor Jaffe, I often thought, Damn, I didn't see that coming.

Dante thought words were either *pexa* or *hirsuta*. Combed or hairy.

So lofty / down to earth. Grand / matter of fact. Combed / hairy . . . High/low.

There are two ways of acquiring a larger and perhaps loftier vocabulary: After Vladimir Nabokov left Russia, he went to Cambridge University. He read *The Song of Igor's Campaign*, a twelfth-century epic in Slavonic, the precursor to Russian. He read the poets of the nineteenth century. He read the Russian writers of natural history. He bought a secondhand copy of Dahl's *Interpretative Dictionary of the Living Russian Language* in four volumes. He read ten pages every night, making notes of words or phrases that particularly pleased him. He confessed that he was driven by the fear that he would lose his Russian, but it's clear that he was also enlarging it. Two decades later he feared that his English prose wouldn't be up to his Russian, but it's clear that he was assiduous.

There is some variant of modesty in his recounting his two fears. I believe his perfectionist fears, but I'm going to add a bit of oral history. Some four decades later—Nabokov's "two decades" plus two—Nabokov was lecturing at Harvard. He said, "There are only two great writers of English for whom English was not their native language. One is Joseph Conrad. I am the other one."

His lordly self-confidence is breathtaking.

The moral of the four-volume-dictionary story is ardor.

Yes, lordly self-confidence. But an ardent devotion to his first language.

What can we speakers and writers of English draw from this example? Do we have to *study* our own language even if we are not refugees from our native country? Is this a necessary or even good way to go? The Poe way?

> Once upon a midnight dreary, while I pondered
> weak and weary,
> Over many a quaint and curious volume of forgotten
> lore.

Nabokov as a small boy had in succession English govern-esses, French governesses, and a Russian tutor. He did master English to perfection, occasionally to an exactitude that makes the reader wrinkle his brow. Here comes a Nabokovian word that stopped me in my tracks. He describes a pet Great Dane examining a snow drift. A bit later he finds a "xanthic hole." Off to the dictionary. It's from Greek, xanthas meaning yellow. So Nabokov is showing off? A bit further in the definition there's this: "xanthic calculus, a urinary calculus containing xanthine." So Nabokov is triumphantly correct. It's not just yellow; it is a hole made by crystallized urine, in this case the Great Dane's.

Speak, Memory is—its dozen elaborate exactitudes notwith-standing—a great work of art and a work that is about how to create art. It is also a story made up of stories, many of which are witty, many of which still make me weep. I'm going to quote a passage I examine in another essay, "Meanwhile Back at the Ranch" but for a different purpose.

It isn't until page 193 that we learn how Vladimir Nabokov's father died. "In 1922 at a public lecture in Berlin my father shielded the lecturer (his old friend Milyukin) from the bullets of the Russian Fascists, and, while rigorously knocking down one of the assassins, was fatally shot by the other." But the following elegy for his father comes earlier.

The old and the new, the liberal touch and the patriarchal one, fatal poverty and fatalistic wealth got fantastically interwoven in that strange first decade of our century. Several times during a summer it might happen that in the middle of luncheon, in the bright, many-windowed, walnut-paneled dining room on the first floor of our Vyra manor, Aleksey, the butler, with an unhappy expression on his face, would bend over and inform my father in a low voice (especially low if we had company) that a group of villagers wanted to see the *barin* outside. Briskly my father would remove his napkin from his lap and ask my mother to excuse him. One of the windows at the west end of the dining room gave upon a portion of the drive near the main entrance. One could see the top of the honeysuckle bushes opposite the porch. From that direction the courteous buzz of a peasant welcome would reach us as the invisible group greeted my invisible father. The ensuing parley, conducted in ordinary tones, would not be heard, as the windows underneath which it took place were closed to keep out the heat. It presumably had to do with a plea for his mediation in some local feud, or with some special subsidy, or with the permission to harvest some bit of our land or cut down a coveted clump of our trees. If, as usually happened, the request was at once granted, there would be again that buzz, and then, in token of gratitude, the good *barin* would be put through the national ordeal of being rocked and tossed up and securely caught by a score or so of strong arms.

In the dining room, my brother and I would be told to go on with our food. My mother, a tidbit between finger and thumb, would glance under the table to see if her nervous and gruff dachshund was there. *"Un jour ils vont le laisser tomber,"* would come from Mlle Golay, a primly pessimistic old lady who had been my mother's governess and still dwelt with us (on awful terms with our own governesses). From my place at table I would suddenly see through one of the west windows a marvelous case of levitation. There, for an instant, the figure of my father in his wind-rippled white summer suit would be displayed, gloriously sprawling in midair, his limbs in a curiously causal attitude, his handsome, imperturbable features turned to the sky. Thrice, to the mighty heave-ho of his invisible tossers, he would fly up in this fashion, and the second time he would go higher than the first and then there he would be, on his last and loftiest flight, reclining, as if for good, against the cobalt blue of the summer noon, like one of those paradisiac personages who comfortably soar, with such a wealth of folds in their garments, on the vaulted ceiling of a church while below, one by one, the wax tapers in mortal hands light up to make a swarm of minute flames in the mist of incense, and the priest chants of eternal repose, and funeral lilies conceal the face of whoever lies there, among the swimming lights, in the open coffin.

I've quoted this passage in another essay. It is worth many readings. In "Meanwhile" it was to illustrate near simultaneity. This time it is for a change in tone. The shift from conversational anecdote to elegy is blurred—the tones overlap. But there are sharp changes in word choice. The vocabulary becomes happily *lyrical* with "my father in his wind-rippled white summer suit" . . . "his handsome imperturbable features turned to the sky." Just after that, a first hint of elegy: "And then there he would be, on his *last* and *loftiest* flight, reclining, *as if for good,* against the cobalt blue of the summer noon." And at last another set of words that transfers the image to "the vaulted ceiling of a church, while below, one by one, the wax tapers in mortal hands light up to make a swarm of minute flames in the mist of incense, and the priest chants of eternal repose, and funeral lilies conceal *the face of whoever* lies there, among the swimming lights, in the open coffin." [Italics added.]

This is an exalted passage from someone whose language was just right for his early life in—for all its flaws—one of the most civilized cultures in the world. When it vanished he had a vocabulary just right for remembering it and for writing an elegy of the father he adored.

A CONTEMPORARY OF Nabokov's, and a fellow Russian, had a different education. Equally smart and equally cosseted (though not on the Nabokov scale), this smart kid with bad eyes ended up in the Red Cavalry in a Cossack regiment. He had to learn a different vocabulary from the one he knew in his youth. There were details about sabers, pistols, and machine guns, but there was also the everyday speech of often illiterate Cossacks.

Here is a letter that Isaac Babel either took down from dictation or in some part created. It is a letter from one of three brothers fighting for the Reds. It is to the boy's mother.

> In the second lines of this letter I hasten to
> describe to you about Dad, that he killed my brother

Theo a year ago. Dad was then with General Denikin[2] . . . And they took us all prisoners . . . And my
brother Theo came to Dad's notice. And Dad began
cutting him about, saying "Brute, Red cur, son of
a bitch" . . . and went on cutting him about until it
grew dark and Theodore passed away . . .

I soon ran away from Dad and got to my unit
under Comrade Pevlichenko. I need to go to my
brother Simon's place to eat pancakes or goose. Then
we began to chase General Denikin and killed thousands of them, and drove them into the Black Sea.

But Simon got Dad all right and he began to whip
Dad. Then Simon splashed water over Dad's beard
and asked him:

"You all right, Dad, in my hands?"

"No," says Dad, "not all right."

Then Simon said, "And Theo, was he all right in
your hands when you killed him?

"No," says Dad." Things went badly for Theo."

Then Simon asked: "And did you think, Dad, that
things would go badly for you?"

"No," says Dad, "I didn't think things would go
badly for me." . . .

[A]nd Simon sent me away so that I can't describe
to you, Dear Mother, how they finished off Dad,
because I was sent off . . .

I remain your loving son, Vasily Timofevich
Kurdyokov

P.S. Mama, do look after [my horse] and God
won't ever abandon you.

---

2. Denikin fought for the Whites in the Red-White Civil War.

In another story Babel is discussing the stories of Guy de Maupassant. Babel writes, "I began to speak of style, of the army of words, of the army in which all kinds of weapons may come into play. No iron can stab the heart with such force as a period put at the right place." Babel learned this from Maupassant. He also learned it from Cossacks.

Here is another passage from an American story many of you will recognize. It is thematically linked in that it describes a son at the moment of his father's death. It is different in that it mixes the high/lofty with the plain idiom of the boy. The boy is fleeing the scene of a crime his father has committed.

Behind him the white man was shouting, "My horse! Fetch my horse!" and he thought for an instant of cutting across the park and climbing the fence into the road, but he did not know the park nor how high the vine-massed fence might be and he dared not risk it. So he ran on down the drive, blood and breath roaring; presently he was in the road again though he could not see it. He could not hear either: the galloping mare was almost upon him before he heard her, and even then he held his course, as if the urgency of his wild grief and need must in a moment more find him wings, waiting until the ultimate instant to hurl himself aside and into the weed-choked roadside ditch as the horse thundered past and on, for an instant in furious silhouette against the stars, the tranquil early summer night sky which, even before the shape of the horse and rider vanished, strained abruptly and violently upward: a long, swirling roar incredible and soundless, blotting the stars, and he springing up and into the road again, running again, knowing it was too late yet still running even after he heard the shot and, an instant later, two shots, pausing now without knowing he had ceased to run,

crying "Pap! Pap!," running again before he knew he had
begun to run, stumbling, tripping over something and scrab-
bling up again without ceasing to run, looking backward over
his shoulder at the glare as he got up, running on among the
invisible trees, panting, sobbing, "Father! Father!"

The conventional advice about describing action is to use
short simple sentences. William Faulkner's sentences here are
neither short nor simple. They are long. They are also as filled
with dependent clauses as an elaborately constructed passage of
classical Latin, yet as hectic as the action.

Near the end of the paragraph the boy cries, "Pap! Pap!" his
usual familiar word. A few lines later he is "panting, sobbing
'Father! Father!'"

"After great pain, a formal feeling comes," Emily Dickinson
noted.

At midnight he was sitting on the crest of a hill. He did not
know it was midnight and he did not know how far he had
come. But there was no glare behind him now and he sat
now, his back toward what he had called home for four days
anyhow, his face toward the dark woods which he would
enter when breath was strong again, small, shaking steadily
in the chill darkness, hugging himself into the remainder of
his thin, rotten shirt, the grief and despair now no longer
terror and fear but just grief and despair. Father. My father,
he thought. "He was brave!" he cried suddenly, aloud but
not loud, no more than a whisper: "He was! He was in the
war! He was in Colonel Sartoris' cav'ry!" not knowing that
his father had gone to that war a private in the fine old European sense, wearing no uniform, admitting the authority of
and giving fidelity to no man or army or flag, going to war

as Malbrouck himself did: for booty—it meant nothing and less than nothing to him if it were enemy booty or his own.

In his own voice the boy cries, "He was brave! . . . He was! He was in the war! He was in Colonel Sartoris' cav'ry!" This is followed by an ironic and elegant authorial intervention: "not knowing that his father had gone to that war as a private in the fine old European sense, wearing no uniform, admitting the authority of and giving fidelity to no man or army or flag." In plainer language, a looter.

The slow constellations wheeled on. It would be dawn and then sun-up after a while and he would be hungry. But that would be tomorrow and now he was only cold, and walking would cure that. His breathing was easier now and he decided to get up and go on, and then he found that he had been asleep because he knew it was almost dawn, the night almost over. He could tell that from the whippoorwills. They were everywhere now among the dark trees below him, constant and inflectioned and ceaseless, so that, as the instant for giving over to the day birds drew nearer and nearer, there was no interval at all between them. He got up. He was a little stiff, but walking would cure that too as it would the cold, and soon there would be the sun. He went on down the hill, toward the dark woods within which the liquid silver voices of the birds called unceasing—the rapid and urgent beating of the urgent and quiring heart of the late spring night. He did not look back.

The final paragraph is elegiac. We are still with the boy but not within his terror or hunkered grief. We are seeing and sensing the boy at a distance, but it's not an ironic or diminishing distance. It starts from very far, while the boy sleeps: "The slow constellations wheeled on." And then almost dawn. "[W]hip-poorwills . . . [A]s the instant for giving over to the day birds drew nearer and nearer, there was no interval at all between them . . . He went on down the hill, toward the dark woods within which the liquid silver voices of the birds called unceas-ing—the rapid and urgent beating of the urgent quiring heart of the late spring night."

This sentence gives relief to the boy, relief to the sympathetic reader. It is also lovely.

"HER TABLE SPREAD" by Elizabeth Bowen is a comedy of manners. I recommend it highly. I also highly recommend the anthology in which I read it—*The Short Story* by Sean O'Faolain. He edited it and wrote instructive commentaries on each story. Edward Weeks, the editor of the *Atlantic Monthly*, gave a copy to James Alan McPherson when McPherson was starting out as a short-story writer. I also recommend McPherson's books of short stories *Hue and Cry* and *Elbow Room*. *Elbow Room* won the Pulitzer Prize for fiction.

"Her Table Spread" is both farcical and witty. It has the *rhythm* of a French farce. It also has an omniscient narrator who operates in another and superior dimension, a narrator com-plicit with the reader. This narrator hovers above the charac-ters, something like Puck but with more formal manners. This arrangement provides high comedy without disturbing the rhythm of the farce.

Part of the farce is that the Anglo-Irish gentlefolk of the house have mistaken their English visitor, Alban. They think he is a suitor for the young lady of the house, Valeria. Valeria is saved from this mistake by her own delusion. She has pinned her hopes on one or another of the officers of a ship of the Royal

Navy now anchored in the estuary. It is a gossamer fantasy spun by this big beautiful woman with the mind of child. The Anglo-Irish characters are all women except for an old uncle with a taste for whiskey and the parlor maid.

The cross-purposes are deftly and wittily deployed, so that it is startling but not surprising that Valeria leaves the dining room in a rush, waving a lantern to signal her imagined Royal Navy suitors. The old uncle enlists Alban to head her off. The two men go to the boathouse. "She's a fine oar," the uncle explains. In the boathouse the uncle uncorks a bottle of whiskey. Alban is terrified by a bat and runs back into the dark. Valeria's lantern has blown out. Two of the women are running down the hill. The two women, Valeria, and Alban bump into each other. Valeria mistakes Alban for a British officer and declares herself. Alban, however, surrounded by women, is briefly but completely shaken out of his Edwardian timidity: "For a moment, without moving or speaking, he stood, in the dark, in a flame, as though all three said: 'My darling . . .'"

There is a pause in Bowen's narration. It is the end of the comedy, but not of the story. Bowen adds several lines of what O'Faolain calls "dilated language":

> Perhaps it was best for them all that early, when next day first lightened the rain, the destroyer steamed out—below the extinguished Castle where Valeria lay with her arms wide, past the boathouse where Mr. Rossiter lay insensible and the bat hung masked in its wings—down the estuary into the open sea.

O'Faolain's commentary in part: "We see, or do not see, an 'extinguished castle' . . . It may be said that such use of language does not make for clarity. It does not. Neither does it make pictures; it is impressionistic . . . Yet in this language some of the wittiest things in English have been written . . . Its value for the short story is: . . . so alert a language helps to make short stories shorter."

Shorter, yes. O'Faolain loves short. But there is a difference between cutting a story short and ending it with a passage that is in its "dilated language" both expansive and concentrated. How can this be? How can a final passage be both expansive and concentrated? In Bowen's final passage it is by distilling the elements of the story—the characters (foolish Valeria and tipsy Mr. Rossiter stand for the rest), the details (let the bat stand for a dozen others), the "castle" (in Ireland this means any great house), and the ship sailing away into the open sea. This isn't just recapitulation. The tone and diction have moved into fuller musical chords, in the same way that Faulkner's "Barn Burning" ends with birds quiring in the same way that Nabokov's elegy for his father moves from the polite lunch table to hearty peasant "heave-ho" to a funeral mass.

All of these passages—and add to them Fitzgerald's ending of *The Great Gatsby*—are lofty in the sense of heightened. They are also "alert" in the sense that O'Faolain means. The story has earned the right to send this last urgent transmission to the reader.

IN OTHER WORDS

Notes on translating. Some surprising effects on one's native language—some playful, some ghostly.

I N KONSTANTIN Stanislavski's book *An Actor Prepares* there are lots of instructions about sense memory, truth onstage, zones of concentration, and focus. They are valuable not only for actors but also, with some translation, for writers. Use what you find in yourself. *How* to use what you are.

It is in an almost casual aside that Stanislavski tells his actors, of course you must also work on the instrument, that is, your physical self. You must take voice lessons, dance lessons, fencing, and gymnastics. When your sense-memory and imagination bring you the true feeling for your part, the instrument must be good enough to project it with clarity and grace.

Our instrument is English. Are there equivalents for sword-play, tumbling, dance, and bel canto? There are a few books about how to get to truth in writing—Vladimir Nabokov's *Speak, Memory* is, among other things, an instructional as well as an exemplary text on becoming an artist. *Portrait of the Artist as a Young Man* is both a celebration of literary ambition and a mockery of it. Ezra Pound's *ABC of Reading* is full of dogma, some vast statements about the nature of good writing, and also some helpful anecdotes about paying attention to the details of the physical world.

But *exercises* for the instrument? Exercises that will increase our clarity and grace? Of course the analyzing of great and not-so-great works by others can have an exercising effect on one's own instrument. There is also sometimes a benefit in earning your bread by doing nonfiction writing. I used to do outdoor-sports writing. My criteria for taking an assignment were, in ascending order, Is the pay good? Is it about a sport or trek I've always wanted to do? And above all, will it involve describing something physical objectively and efficiently so that the nonfiction writing will be like a charcoal sketch of something that I *might* use later? That I might use, so to speak, in a more ambitious oil painting, where the physical will also have emotional resonance? That last bit—the charcoal sketch—may have two elements. The first is putting into words a physical thing or act. The second is acquiring the technical vocabulary, whether it's wine tasting or downhill skiing, and translating it for the general reader. Both are forms of translating—and in a way all writing is translating. You bring something across.

That's the windup. Here's the pitch. What about translating in the most common sense of the word—from one language to another?

At first blush you might think it's a good way to learn—or to improve your knowledge of—a foreign language. Strange to say, it's not. Translating will increase your *admiration* of a foreign language. It will *improve* your English. If you're really doing your job, it'll take you right back home.

I was talking over my translation of the next-to-last chapter of an Italian novel with the author—some stuff about the difference between bobby pins and hairpins, distinct words that I now know in English but have forgotten in Italian. I said, "We've got time to get to the end. Shall we do the last chapter?"

"Oh, John, I can't," she said. "It always makes me cry." A pause. "Did it make you cry?"

"Yes," I said. "When I read it in English."

She laughed and laughed.

For lots of reasons, but one of them was our surprise that, after all our friendship and admiration in Italian, I really *live* in English.

Here are some short take-home exercises. Lorenzo Da Ponte wrote the lyrics for Mozart's Italian operas. A lot of opera lyrics are disappointing. Da Ponte's aren't. And in *The Marriage of Figaro* he was working from a very good play in French by Beaumarchais. Cherubino, a page in the count's household, has a crush—crushes—on the Countess and Figaro's fiancée Susanna. The count finally has enough of Cherubino and decides to send him off to the army. Figaro sings an aria, the tune of which you've probably heard lots of times. Figaro is gleefully mocking Cherubino:

> Non più andrai, farfallone amoroso,
> Notte e giorno d'interno girando,
> Delle belle turbando il riposo,
> Narcisetto, Adoncino d'amor.

Farfella is butterfly. Narcisso is Narcissus (the one who was so beautiful he fell in love with his own reflection). Adono is

Adonis—a male beauty. The translation problem is in the suffixes. *One* when added to a noun almost always gives a sense of something ungainly. There's Federico Fellini's movie—*I Vitelloni*. *Vitello* means "calf." Fellini's movie is about ungainly young men roistering around in a small town. *I Vitelloni.* All this insult is tucked into the suffix.

Narcisetto, Adoncino: usually diminutive suffixes (*etto, ino*) are endearing. But as with the English *little*, they can also have a deflating, even a nasty, sense. "Why, you little sneak." But Figaro's words are hard to translate without running out of space.

> You won't go anymore, amorous butterfly
> Fluttering around inside night and day
> Disturbing the sleep of beauties,
> A little Narcissus and Adonis of love.

That translation is more or less word for word. One of two rusty old saws about translation comes to mind. "A translation is like a mistress: either beautiful or faithful." "You amorous butterfly" is faithful.

Try it. See if you can work in a sense of ungainliness. Maybe *lovesick moth*? Maybe *flapping* instead of *fluttering*? You have to take some liberties.

We used to have diminutive endings in English. A small cod was a codling. As in Orlando Gibbons's musical piece "Crys of London": "Hot codlings, hot!" Now in Boston it's scrod. A little prince was a princeling. In *The Hobbit* and *The Lord of the Rings* the hobbits are doubly diminished: halfling. Won't work with Narcissus.

Here's a shorter exercise. It's a boast in Latin that occurs in Renaissance Italy and was on the badge of a Scottish clan, the McGregor's I think. *Nemo me impune lacessit.* Easy. No one harms me with impunity. My problem, and it may only be mine, is that when I hear "harms me with impunity" I suddenly see impunity as a great big club. I set this sentence before an undergraduate class. "Nobody messes with me." Some added, "And gets away with it." A lot of words for a single one—*impune*—but it has some tang to it. The old revolutionary flag showing a rattlesnake and the motto "Don't tread on me" is an efficient equivalent. One kid, more at home on city streets than in the woods observing birds, came up with "You fuck with the falcon, you get the fang." A +, though I'm still hoping for something concise and venerable.

Here's one that looks easy but has a snag in it:

> ¿Qué piensa el cerdo de la aurora?
> No cantan pero la sostienen
> con sus grandes cuerpos rosados
> con sus pequeñas patas duras
>
> Los cerdos sostienen la aurora.
> . . .
> Quiero conversar con los cerdos.

Literal translation:

> What does the pig think about the dawn?
> They do not sing but they sustain it
> With their big rose bodies
> With their little hard feet.

It's the *sostienen* that's hard. *Sustain* seems to me to include a sense of nourishment. Sustenance. Maybe it does in Spanish. I don't know Spanish. It also means "support." Not a great choice. And if you go for the chattier *hold up*, there's the chance that someone will hear it as meaning *hold back*. Maybe "carry the dawn"?

I think the poem in Spanish is meant to sound conversational, a remark someone is making over his shoulder to the person out on a walk with him around the farm. But there are sound patterns—those *a*s and *e*s—in the first line. The *a*s in the second. And then a rush of *s*'s. *Rosados* and *patas duras*—hard paws. Neither roseate nor rose is an everyday word in English as it is in Italian, French, and—I'm extrapolating—Spanish. So *pink*. Pigs don't have paws; *hooves* is just too hard to say right. Okay, feet. Little hard feet. *T*, *d*, *t* come down nicely from the large pink bodies, as does the Spanish.

The point is how we have to rummage through the sounds of our English. (Some of you who have known some pigs may cock an eyebrow at the pink pig. The pigs I've seen—Chester White, Hampshire, Poland-China—weren't pink. Porky Pig is pink. But we'll let that pass.)

A short parenthetical example of haste in translation. One of my many uncles lived in Paris. The French, unlike the Italians, didn't use to dub films but relied on subtitles. My uncle swore he saw a Western movie in Paris with the following exchange in a saloon.

"Howdy, pardner." Subtitle: *Enchanté.*
"Gimme a shot of red-eye." *Un apéritif, s'il vous plait.*

I hope it's true. An Italian would say, *"Se non è vero, è ben trovato."* Literally: "If it's not true it's well found." Or: "If it's not true, it ought to be."

It occurs to me that you don't *have* to be dealing with a foreign language to do your exercise. There's English and there's

English. English, for various historical reasons, has absorbed foreign vocabularies. *Veau* in French means "calf" *or* "veal." And we have sheep *and* mutton. There's cow or steer and beef. There's hen or chicken and pullet (though you don't hear that much anymore). Pig and pork. After the Normans conquered England, the Anglo-Saxon peasants raised the calf, but when it was served to the Norman lord in his castle it was *veau*, or veal. And so forth. *Mouton, boeuf, poulet* . . .

English has also absorbed turns of phrase, odd constructions that come from the languages that knuckled under to the English conquerors and colonizers. An Anglo-Irish gentlewoman had to learn what is probably an element of Irish grammar. She says, "Seamus, have you hoed the rose bed?" He says, "I'm just after doing it, ma'am." He's saying that it's done but quaintly enough so that he might be meaning "I'm just fixin' to do it."

ONE MORE THOUGHT about Irish-English. There are still a few bardic rhythms. One summer long, long ago, my friend Steve Truitt and I were selling our bodies to science, and we ended up in a NASA-sponsored experiment at Mass General Hospital, administered by two doctors, one from Tennessee, the other from Ireland. Truitt and I got to be friends with them, and before submitting to the pain experiment, sometimes with morphine, sometimes not, we'd eat lunch with the doctors. Truitt said, "Look—here we are getting to be pals. Isn't that going to spoil your scientific objectivity?"

The Irish doctor said, "Not at all, at all. Here you come, Truitt, suffering from acute alcohol poisoning and postcoital amnesia, and we use you as the lowest common denominator."

Like the river Liffey rippling out with the ebb tide.

*   *   *

A WORD ABOUT false friends. Words like *largo*, meaning "wide" in Italian but "long" in Spanish. *Fastidious* in English means "picky," but in Italian it means "annoying." A small child in a schoolyard says, *"Maestra, Paolo mi da fastidio!"* (Teacher, Paolo gives me annoyance.)

When I was just getting to know the Ferri family, it was the summer of 1991. Linda Ferri, the writer whose novel I later translated, rushed into the dining room. She'd heard some news from her husband, a French diplomat in Rome. To be sure I understood, she spoke in English: "Gorbachev is destitute!"

I was puzzled—should we pass the hat for the poor guy? It turned out that *destituito* in Italian means "overthrown" or "dismissed from office."

More recently, my friend Giuseppe was entertaining three Kentucky ladies. He'd been asked by a friend to show them Rome. He spent the day with them and brought them to his house to cook them an Italian meal. A sweet, obliging man. He telephoned me and said, "Please come. My little English is exhausted. You can help me entertain them and be so kind as to translate." A soon as I got there, he disappeared into the kitchen to catch his breath. After a bit he popped out to say in English, "I hope you all like handkerchiefs."

Puzzlement. He turned to me and said, *"Carcioffi."* Artichokes.

You can hear what he'd done. The two English words as well as the Italian all sound like a sneeze.

Linda Ferri's novel is called *Incantesimi* in Italian. The *Oxford Italian Dictionary* says it means "spells." Won't do in American. Enchantments—okay, let it go at that. My fourteen-year-old daughter, even though she had no idea that spells are to this day more serious in Italy than in America, said "Incantations." Yes.

I called my editor. Good. But then she called back. The new sales force said, "That's not a word in everyone's vocabulary." Enough to make you weep.

Linda Ferri was editing an Italian translation of Peter Taylor's stories. She and I were comparing the English and Italian. In one story a flirtatious aunt is telling someone not to move to Saint Louis. She says, "I've been to St. Louis, see what it done done to me."

"*Ma perchè* 'done done,'" Linda said. "*Che vuol dire?*"

I said, "She's joking. It's southern dialect. See what you done made me do. What you gone done now? Boy, what you done done to her? There's a bunch of songs . . ."

"Oh," she said. "*Canta mela*. Sing it to me."

Sometimes translating reminds us that there are untranslatable words or idioms that push us into finding not just a word but a whole roundabout phrase that finds the feeling. Other times translation reminds us that all these words are sounds made by the mouths of our fellow earthlings—and there are times you float for an instant in a pre–Tower of Babel air and then glide back to earth to your English, perhaps improved by travel.

Russia in a nutshell. Alexander Pushkin, summing up the difference between Russia and western Europe, said, "The Arabs brought you Aristotle and algebra. The Mongols brought us taxation and the whip." Alexander Blok in his poem "The Scythians" says to Europe, "You are millions. We are shadows, shadows, shadows." He goes on to say, "And yet we smell the far-off scent of lemon groves." *Limónikh roshch dalyóki aromát.*

However, St. Petersburg (as it was, and is again) was a great European city with its own scents. In 1913 it published more books than the United States did in 1952. There were Dmitri

Mendeleev, Ivan Pavlov, Sergei Diaghilev, Nikolai Rimsky-Korsakov and lots of poets, the silver age of poets.

Here's a bit of another Alexander Blok poem, this one about individual despair rather than epic dreams. It attracted the attention of Rainer Maria Rilke, and a friend of his, so I've heard, translated it into German. It occurs to me it might have been Lou Andreas-Salomé. She got around, traveled to Russia. I only know a little Russian and pretty much no German, but the ingenuity of Rilke's friend (whether the story is true or not doesn't matter for our purpose) is audible. I heard both versions when I was twenty-one and I'm doing them from memory—the Blok would be easy to refind, but if anyone can track down the German I'd be grateful.

Весенний день прошел без дела
У неумытого окна;
Скучала за стеной и пела,
Как птица пленная, жена.

Я, не спеша, собрал бесстрастно
Воспоминанья и дела;
И стало беспощадно ясно:
Жизнь прошумела и ушла.

Еще вернутся мысли, споры,
Но будет скучно и темно;
К чему спускать на окнах шторы?
День догорел в душе давно.

Spring day passed without incident
Outside unwashed window.
Was being bored on other side of wall
And was singing like captive bird, wife.

I, not hurrying, gathered memories and deeds . . .
And it became indefensibly clear
Life [untranslatable, maybe "noised away"] and left.

The first part is pretty straightforward.

Der frühling Tag wergang wie immer
[something something] Fenster ungeputst und grau.

The translator has added "gray" to the unwashed window. Okay. In the next part—"gathered memories"—she or he had good luck with the beautiful Russian for memories—*vospomeenánya*. The German is beautiful too—*Erinnerungen*.

The last two lines of that stanza in German:

Es war unerbíttlich Klar
Das Leben ist vorbeígeshaumt.

With *unerbíttlich*, the translator gave up the notion of "defenseless," but *unerbíttlich* doesn't just mean merciless—it sounds merciless. Harsh but close enough to the meaning. And the translator kept the four-syllable rhythm of *besposhchadno*.

For *proshoomyéla i ooshlá* she/he wrote *vorbeígeshaumt. Shaum* means "foam." This past participle is prolonged by two glued-in initial prepositions so that it has the splash and retreat of a wave.

When I was twenty-one, a teacher set the exercise of translating the poem into English, using both the Russian and the German. The teacher may have heard Ezra Pound's advice to young poets: Listen to poems in languages you don't know. Listen to the sound. I'm glad to say I've lost my attempt. Something about a candle guttering. Too small and finicky, as if I were poking at something with an umbrella tip, not using my bare hands.

But the sounds and the meaning of the sounds keep coming back. I have a little cabin on the upper Delaware River, up on a twenty-foot bank. In the spring of 2005, the Delaware rose twenty-six feet. I wasn't there. A brother-in-law sent me a videotape of the river flowing through the cabin. I got there later to join a plumber and a carpenter. One said to the other, "Do you want to tell him or shall I? Okay—it's not just the floor joists, it's the rim joist, and it's not just the rim joist, it's the base plate."

The river was flowing peacefully again—flowing by where we stood, on down past Milford township, Dingman's Ferry, the Delaware Water Gap, past Trenton, past Philadelphia, into Delaware Bay and then the sea. All that was as ever. The upstream side of the cabin and the inside of the single main room were plastered with silt as fine as talc. It was distressing. Also amazingly lovely. The bushes and trees on the downstream side were decorated with a canoe-paddle blade, a page of a bird book, an upstream neighbor's propane tank and shed door. Part of me was thinking insurance claim, FEMA, and new pump for the well, but a tiny bit of me was spellbound by the ankle-high silt on the part of the floor still there, the inch of silt face high on the walls. It felt like silk, but it turned to smoke between my fingers.

I wasn't consciously thinking of *vospomeenánya* or *proshoomyéla i ooshlá* then, and nothing may come of the river silt after all—there may be no missing word under the debris—but soon I did begin to move toward the poem. My bare hand was touching something that began to disrupt the order of the usual word for thing. My English still can't find the note. There is the liquid sound of Russian and a gurgling of not-quite-right English noises. There is the aftermath of river silt. There is a sense of things carried away, of things running out, and the bleakness after.

And then the touch of silt set off another echo. I loved my first father-in-law. I spent a lot of time with him. He and his wife transformed an old barn in Rhode Island into a huge summer-house, filled for ten summers with family, three generations, at times seventeen of us, and I can say that there was a time when we all loved one another. My father-in-law covered the ground floor with cork tiles. Because they were laid on top of an old concrete slab they curled up with damp. He then ordered elegant terra-cotta tiles in the shape of fleur-de-lis and had them laid in with grout. The interlacing fleur-de-lis were indeed elegant, but the rising-damp problem recurred and walking on them made the tiles slip and grind. We all learned to walk softly and the tiles stayed in place. My father-in-law died fairly young, age sixty. All four of his children divorced. His widow finally had to sell the house. Before the new owner moved in, and while everything in the house was still there, the propane tank exploded and the house burned—not all the way down but halfway. A while later I was in Rhode Island again, doing some work, and I realized I was near the old house. Will it be too much after all? Let's see. The bay-facing half was gone except for the three-story-high chimney. The vast living room where we'd played murder in the dark was gone. I walked around outside. The flower beds and vegetable garden I'd planted were all weeds. I was okay, just taking things in. I went around back. The outside door to the corner room where my first two daughters had slept was open. Their twin beds were still there, the bedspreads covered with gray ash. I was defended against that. I went into the hall past the bedroom where my then wife and I had slept. I turned into the ground-floor front hall, wading through the layer of ashes. The walls here were scorched but still standing. There was a large silence. The silence made me stop. I took another step. I moved my foot sideways, brushing ashes aside. I saw the red fleur-de-lis tiles. I touched them. They were *at last* perfectly set.

Then I felt what was gone. All of it, all at once.

I heard Blok's poem when I was twenty-one. I saw the red tiles when I was forty-two. Another twenty-odd years later, the silt and thinking about translation brought all these things together. I didn't find the missing *proshoomyéla*, but instead *another* word in Blok's last two lines became heavier and clearer. *Besposhchadno*. Without defense.

Is there a moral to this side story? Maybe this: there are things and there are words—sometimes *meaning* is a solid link, but sometimes meaning is a ghost that waits and waits until an accident brings it howling silently into you.

NEIGHBORHOODS

An appreciation of Hubert Butler, one of the great and underappreciated writers of the twentieth century.

Tip O'Neill (former Speaker of the House, D-MA), American Irish, said "All politics is local." Gruff and brilliant.

Hubert Butler, Anglo-Irish, is elegant and brilliant about how much more than politics is local.

IN THE summer of 1979 there was a postal strike in Ireland, which also meant that the telephone service was out. This was an inconvenience, of course, but it also meant that when I drove to Maidenhall to drop off one or the other of Hubert Butler's grand-daughters (who occasionally helped take care of my two very young daughters) and Hubert asked me in for tea, there were no phone calls—and so we could talk and talk. A visitor from America forgets how far north Ireland is and how long the summer daylight lasts. I often left with a book Hubert thought I should read and eventually, near the end of my stay, with a folder of his own essays. The first sentence from the folder: "I have lived for most of my life on the Nore and own three fields upon its banks, some miles before it turns to the southeast and forces its way under Brandon Hill to join the Barrow above New Ross." It rings just right. Clear and confident—confident but without egotism—the initial "I" soon becomes the mind's eye that follows the river as it makes its way to join the Barrow. The sentence stops short of the sea. The subject of the essay is the neighborhood, not the world.

Mind's eye and neighborhood—the good twins of so many of Butler's essays. But the second essay in the folder was about Butler's long term as an English teacher in Leningrad in 1931. Is there a contradiction here? Is this allegiance to neighborhood, to the local and human scale of things at risk? I think not, but it is interesting to see how Butler is consistent and clear in what he values most.

Butler went for a brief visit and made what appears to be a spur-of-the-moment decision to stay on. He shared a small flat with a Russian friend, the friend's mother, and several other people. He sets up a camp cot between the stove and the window. He doesn't explain his motives and scarcely mentions his misgivings. It is only by way of some by-the-way sentences we learn that he already speaks Russian: "Over the whole flat there was that sweetish musty smell of black bread and benzine and scent and galoshes that Russians seem to carry with them, even into exile. I felt lonely and ill at ease. Nina Gavrilovna [the friend's mother] plainly did not want me there. She refused to believe that being foreign I could understand anything, unless she shouted at me with plentiful gesticulations." Almost all the details about material life are bleak and daunting, but Butler's bright interest in everyone he meets is evident from his sympathetic but clear-eyed summaries of their life stories.

Christopher Isherwood, who was in Berlin in the thirties in a somewhat similar situation, wrote of his own attitude: "I am a camera with its shutter open." This is true of Butler, perhaps even truer—Butler's account is more about the pictures than about the emotional life of the camera.

Butler isn't neutral—not in the sense of indifferent—but he carefully allows others to make the large statements. At a tea party given by his friend Kolya he meets Baroness Garatinsky. He has learned from Kolya that "[s]he had been an old revolutionary and in 1917 her peasants, who had taken over her estates in Central Russia, had made her their manager. Five years later her position had become impossible and she was now teaching languages in Leningrad . . . In Goskurs where she taught she was the victim of petty persecution. 'Women are the worst,' [Kolya] said."

The baroness, just coming in, hears this:

> She paused in the doorway, leaning on her stick, and diverted with a smile [Kolya's mother's] effort to introduce us and give her a chair. "Later, later, Nina Gavrilovna." To us she said, "Women are allowed a bit more license because even here they aren't taken seriously. Masculine unreliability matters more . . ."

Kolya's mother tries to divert the dangerous conversation: "The baroness, seeing her agitation, said to me, 'You mustn't think that because we have much to complain of we are enemies of the Revolution. The Revolution had to happen, it was the result of generations of suffering and plotting. It is a historical fact, a great convulsion of human nature. If we are to go on living we must accept it, and I have always done so gladly.'"

After that declaration by the baroness we hear no further overview of the Revolution. Well, a word or two—through clenched teeth. This is partly because, now that the last tourist ships of summer have left, Butler is living inside the Revolution, and life is overcoats, galoshes, documents, and food.

Butler sees more of the baroness as the months go by, and he also meets a lot of other people and becomes entwined in their lives. Usually the subject of conversation is immediate necessity, but occasionally there is a sudden beam of light on how the whole Soviet system works, but the beam is generated by a particular situation.

> One day as [Kolya and I] were queuing up outside the office of the Lensoviet, he tried to explain himself to me: "I am a Caucasian from Georgia like Stalin, with the same theological background. He was a theological student. He believes like the Manicheans that there is Good and evil, Black and White, a dichotomy. All this which he thinks Good is Evil." He waved his hand at the Lensoviet and the long queue . . .
>
> I found his claim to be Caucasian as irritating as he found my claim to be Irish . . .
>
> After a pause he said, "Darya Andreyevna . . . thinks you are a spy and wants the house committee to turn you out. She has been to the Upravdom. Lyubotchka did her best for you. She said she thought you were a harmless idiot because you smile when you talk to her."
>
> "I only meant to be friendly."
>
> "Yes, but real Russians only smile at jokes."

There is no apparent ideology in the thirty-year-old Butler nor in the older man who wrote the essay, though his attentiveness to personal character and, sometimes, more largely to Russian characteristics as they blend with or modify Soviet life, is a stance, a corrective to mechanical abstraction.

Darya Andreyevna's husband, it turns out, had been a colonel in the tsar's army and she a famous opera singer.

> After the Revolution she had sung Soviet songs and had been awarded the rank of *naoochnaya rabotnitsa* or scientific worker. Because of this she had first-category food rations . . . she could get, among other things, macaroni. Nina Gavrilovna could never forgive her this. A Tsarist colonel's wife got macaroni while her son, a Marxist professor . . . , had to live on vegetable marrow. Incessantly nagging Kolya about this, she made it psychologically impossible for him to get a first-category food ticket . . . Whenever macaroni was mentioned, his face went dead and cold and Manichean.

With such shrewdness and sympathy Butler takes us through the fall and winter. As Neal Ascherson writes in the foreword to *In the Land of Nod*, Butler is "interested in the 'epiphanies' which make currents of social and political change visible through the lens of some small accident or absurdity."

In the passage from Manicheans to macaroni—from Stalin's Georgian and theological slant and Kolya's rebuttal, to the new privileges and resentments of the classless society at ground level, and then on to the sad truth about a mother's nagging—there is a reversal of the usual ascension of literary magnitude. Instead of lyric, dramatic, and epic, we get epic, dramatic, and lyric.

A great deal is said and more implied in this next short paragraph:

> One day, as I was walking to my classes in the twilight, I saw a large leather-coated figure lying on the pavement. He had an open dispatch case beside him with papers scattered about. He was snoring. A woman came from the far side of

the Moika river to help me lift him up. "What a shame," she exclaimed, "to see such a beautiful coat lying in the mud." We examined it together. "I bet he's a commissar!" she said. "One can only get a coat like that with *valuta*." [Valuta is foreign money]. We dragged him to the Mariinsky Theatre and propped him up sitting against one of the columns of the portico—I told her I had *valuta* and needed a coat, so she took a piece of paper out of his dispatch case and wrote the name of the place where I could get one like it.

Butler, by the way, never does get a coat like it.

Aside from the brisk matter-of-factness of style and aside from the woman's comically fast remark "I bet he's a commissar," there are two other neatnesses of observation.

The first thing the woman says is not what a shame to see a drunk man in the middle of the sidewalk but what a shame to see such a beautiful coat lying in the mud. First things first. And then the odd reminder of the elegance of the once and future St. Petersburg—the columns of the portico of the Mariinsky Theatre.

The essay is filled with passages of such visual and audible clarity, and not only from 1931. Butler modestly holds back until the essay is half over his knowledge and appreciation of Russian literature and history as it has sprung from or been at odds with St. Petersburg or Leningrad. And it becomes clear that he has absorbed and been absorbed by the city. I think that it was not simply his knowledge of the Russian language and Russian literature that made this possible. Nor was it simply his temperament, his quality of sympathetic attentiveness, though that counts for a lot. I think he could not have learned and appreciated so much of another place had he not first educated and enlarged his sense of place at home. And I think he had developed in Ireland a notion of life that is both an element of his style and worldview. No, not worldview—a worldview is a perspective from afar and may be an ideological siren song offering final answers. Butler was skeptical of siren songs and final answers. In our correspondence the subject of what our parents had taught us came up. I had written that my mother lullabied me along the lines of the world-is-your-oyster optimism. Hubert wrote back, "My parents led me to believe that life is a series of minor duties, most of them unpleasant." He may have been led to believe this, and it may have lingered, but as it turned out his sense of duty was not minor, and if understanding is the highest pleasure, he had that too.

But a major element in his belief was that it is necessary to see as much as possible face-to-face, that the epic must be on a realistic human scale.

In the epilogue to the essay Butler returns to Russia in 1956. Between 1931 and 1956 there were the Yezhovshchina—the purges of the mid-1930s—then the war, the bombardment, and the nine-hundred-day siege of Leningrad. His Intourist guide, Anna, supplements his own knowledge.

To the north I saw the islands where I had walked with Yegunov and his dog. They were now called the Kirov Islands, and the great highway that led to them was called Kirov Avenue. Thousands of honest men and women died because of Kirov, but their names are nowhere recorded.

I have forgotten much of what Anna told me but I am more inclined to apologize for writing about great events, which touched me not at all, than for tracing again the tiny snail track which I made myself. I was thinking not of the tremendous disasters that had befallen Leningrad and all Russia, but of the small stupidities, the acts of laziness or

greed I had committed myself. Why had I not given the blue
rug to Kolya's mother instead of leaving it behind by mistake? Why hadn't I sent Guzelimian his fishing rod?

The essay ends with these small self-reproachful questions. I
believe in Butler's immediate confessional pangs, but I certainly
wouldn't assign him more than a very small penance. What I
believe in and accept more completely is the perspective he cre-
ates. There is a similar insistence on scale and perspective in the
essay "The Children of Drancy." The essay is not just about the
Nazi deportation and killing of 4,051 Jewish children in 1942. It
is about the response: "The facts are bleak and few . . . But no
one seems interested. I believe we are bored because the scale
is so large that the children seem to belong to sociology and sta-
tistics. We cannot visualize them reading Babar books, having
their teeth straightened, arranging dolls' tea parties."

When Butler writes of the real details of his Russian friends'
lives or of the imagined details of the unlived lives of the children
of Drancy, he refuses either to let them be reduced to statistical
miniatures or to let them be swept up into the blurred majesty of
epic. What Butler does is to write so well about particulars that
they fix themselves in memory: the overcoat, the wave of Kolya's
hand at the Lensoviet, the macaroni. Small things—but they
become "ciphers to this great account"—a record not only of
themselves but intimating other—so many other—unrecorded
incidents that are the threads of our most necessary history.

CHILDHOOD READING

A recollection of reading. "What's your favor-
ite book?" and "What book has influenced you the
most?" are impossible questions.
    Remembering what you've read is interesting;
remembering how *you've read is a petite madeleine.*

A WHILE AGO I was asked, along with a hundred or so other
American writers, to list the three or four books that most
influenced my writing. I thought and thought. There was
that year with Marcel Proust in which I became simultane-
ously dreamy and nervous, drowsing in the late afternoon and
mentally fluttering at night. And Anton Chekhov and Flannery
O'Conner and Frank O'Connor and Ernest Hemingway, F.
Scott Fitzgerald, William Faulkner, and Stendahl. Honoré de
Balzac and Anatole France. Charles Dickens, George Eliot, Jane
Austen, Charlotte and Emily Brontë. And   Herman Melville

and Nathaniel Hawthorne and don't forget Leo Tolstoy, Fyodor Dostoevsky, Nikolai Gogol—a list of great books. James Joyce and Gustave Flaubert. Miguel de Cervantes.

I didn't major in English in college, so I spent some years after college and law school in what I thought was canonical catching up.

But the truth is that the deepest and oldest and most overwhelming reading came before I became the way I am now.

I REMEMBER A science-fiction novel by Arthur C. Clarke (author of *2001*). This novel is called *Childhood's End*. Early on, a father is lying on a beach with his son. The son is scratching the father's back. Without a word spoken the son moves from itch to itch, scratching with just the right pressure. It is a perfect back scratch. The father realizes the son is reading his mind, and that the son is one of the mutants who must . . . save the earth. And so on.

In *High Couch of Silistra*, Janet Morris (an ecological feminist sci-fi writer) adapts this idea. Silistra is a dry planet, something like the planet in *Dune*. Women rule the few oases. The male caravan leaders, in order to get water, must submit to the women rulers of the oases, be a slave for the night. But if the caravan leader is polite and attractive, the night he spends with the oasis-ruler is bliss, because she can use her ESP to give him the sexual equivalent of the perfect back scratch, as invented by Clarke in *Childhood's End*.

In Janet Morris's subsequent work, a series of which I only remember two—*Cruiser Dreams* and *Earth Dreams*—the women have a psychic power that is even more powerful than that of the oasis rulers of Silistra. Certain women, highly trained in their esoteric art, can induce sleep in their clients and then stimulate and guide the sleeper's dreams so that the dreamer dreams more vividly and deeply than ever before.

As is so often the case, science fiction has not boldly gone where none have dared to go before, but it has produced a metaphor for a hypnotic pleasure and fulfillment we already have on earth—books.

When I was twenty-six I tried to make a list of all the books I'd read. The books from ages six to thirteen I remembered by remembering places. For example: summer afternoon, pine trees, blueberry bushes by the long lake where my grandparents ran a camp for girls. I see the boulder near the front porch of the main lodge, the steps, the dark interior, the huge stone fireplace, the varnished slabs of pine on which are painted names of former campers (my mother, Constance Dudley, 1924; my oldest sister, Jane Casey, 1944), and in the darkest corner, the bookshelf. *Old Mother West Wind*, *Uncle Wiggily*, *Nancy Drew*, *Junior Miss*, *Anne of Green Gables*—I loved these books. I had no desire to escape from this all-girl zone. And yet I remember sometime before I was twelve I paddled a canoe to the end of the lake, camped out alone, and read *I, the Jury* by Mickey Spillane by the light of the kerosene lantern.

At twenty-six in a very cold farmhouse in Iowa wearing two pairs of pants and three sweaters I next remembered Christmases and birthdays and the gifts of books suitable for boys. *Howard Pyle's Book of Pirates*, Robert Louis Stevenson's *The Black Arrow* and *Kidnapped*. *Storm Canvas* by Armstrong Sperry. Lots of science fiction. *The St. Nicholas Anthology*—actually there were two of them, one in Christmas green and one in Christmas red, the best of the *St. Nicholas* magazine, which my mother had read as a girl. An older cousin who was a navy pilot gave me a World War II navy survival manual suitable for crash landings in the Arctic, South Pacific, and the Sahara; each section a starter kit for a daydream story. My father liked Sherlock Holmes. He used to tell us Sherlock Holmes stories when we were very small, many of which he made up. Sometime after World War II I listened to Sherlock Holmes on the radio. I misheard the announcer. I thought he said, "Sherlock Holmes Radio Theater . . . brought to you by Sir Arthur Coal and Oil." When I finally got the book I thought how clever the coal and oil company had been to pick a writer whose name so resembled their own.

But the best source of reading I remembered was Lowdermilk's used-book store downtown in Washington. I think I discovered it when I was in sixth grade. A perfect Friday afternoon for fifty cents—twenty-five cents for a movie, which included a stage show (I once heard Basil Rathbone recite Elizabeth Barret Browning at Loew's Palace or perhaps one of the other Loew's, and Basil Rathbone followed the Harmonicats, a group of harmonica players who performed on roller skates), and I still had twenty-five cents for Lowdermilk's. *All Quiet on the Western Front* by Erich Maria Remarque. Fifteen cents. And only a dime for *A German Deserter's War Experience* by, I later realized, a socialist-pacifist. Why World War I when World War II was the war of my infancy, the war that was in every movie theater? Was it because I couldn't possibly doubt that war but was troubled by the untroubled Technicolor versions? I give myself too much credit for conscience; I suspect I just wanted to know stuff about war that my friends didn't.

It was at Lowdermilk's that I found my own Edgar Rice Burroughs. My father had read Tarzan to us, but I was more taken by the Mars books. *Thuvia, Maid of Mars*. What a lovely title. What sweet infatuation.

At Lowdermilk's I found Rafael Sabatini, stylistically a step up from Burroughs. The opening line of *Scaramouche* is elegant: "Born with the gift of laughter and a sense that the world is mad—that was his only patrimony." Years later I heard that when the Yale residential colleges were built, the architect had inscribed that sentence over one of the gates, without the author's name. Professors of Greek and Latin, of medieval French and neoclassical English were called in to identify the quotation and came up blank. I hope that story is true.

Rafael Sabatini—*Captain Blood, The King's Minion, The Strolling Saint,* and many more. Samuel Shellabarger—*Prince of Foxes, Lord Vanity, Captain from Castille.* Adventure, romance, triumph.

In the cold farmhouse in Iowa I spent two days in that sort of dreamy remembering. The next place I remembered reading was on an airplane. The transatlantic drone of propellers. I was thirteen. *Cry, the Beloved Country* by Alan Paton, a book that turned out to be in the library of the school I was bound for, but which, like the school, was in French—*Pleure, ô Pays Bien-Aimé,* a translation that promised a lot for the sound of the language in which I was abruptly immersed. Two years of *cahiers de dictée,* a Pelikan fountain pen that gave me a blue-black callus on the left side of my right-hand middle finger, and eventually enough fluency to read Alphonse Daudet, Marcel Pagnol, and some of Jean-Jacques Rousseau's reveries. There were also some books in English in the library. A. J. Cronin (very Catholic), Sinclair Lewis, Jack London. During those two years I kept a list of what I read, with checkmarks—one for okay, four for wonderful. I still had that list in Iowa. I now remember seeing that I'd given P. G. Wodehouse's *Carry On, Jeeves* and Arthur Koestler's *Darkness at Noon* four checkmarks each. At fourteen I was equally eager for pleasure and improvement. Of course, *Darkness at Noon* isn't—or wasn't for me—only about Soviet politics and purges. At least one remembered passage arcs across the forty-four-year gap. The communist hero is imprisoned. An old White Russian cavalry officer is in an adjoining cell, has been there for years. The two prisoners communicate by tapping messages in a code, the "quadratic alphabet." The cavalry officer asks whether the new prisoner has had any recent sexual experience. The new prisoner taps back, letter by letter, "She had breasts that would fit into champagne goblets and thighs like a wild mare's."

The truth is that the new prisoner has had no recent sexual experience and sends the message out of charity. That didn't matter to me. In a Swiss all-boy boarding school I was as avid as the old cavalry officer, and like him, I wondered what miracle of time or deliverance would ever bring me to the fevers of that sentence.

There were more fevers from a novel by Anatole France which was not part of French class. *Thaïs*, a story of an Egyptian courtesan and an anchorite. I remember one of the schoolmasters coming into our bedroom to turn out the lights. He spotted *Thaïs*. I looked guilty. He laughed. I looked startled. He said, "I laugh. I laugh because I know you and I know what's in that book." ("*Je ris. Je ris parce que je te connais . . .*" He may even have addressed me as "*mon pauvre petit Casey.*") This Gallic attitude was fortunately shared by the Jesuit priest who came every other week to confess us.

I gradually but definitely had left stage one—reading with innocent gluttony. But I wasn't just looking for fevers. Even the swashbucklers weren't just escape. All this reading was a jumble of daydreams and language that gave off notions, possible formulations about the grown-up world outside the schoolroom and the church. It was a swirl of vapors that was not given off by my life or anyone's that I could see, but I thought it must come from somewhere wonderful and that these vapors came from the forms and heats of the best sort of grown-up life. This is an intoxicating and dangerous kind of reading. It is the kind of reading that Emma Bovary did in *her* schooldays and that gave her a synthetic imagination that filled her with unfulfillable yearnings. But I imagine that what makes Madame Bovary so much more than a cautionary tale is that Flaubert had done the same sort of reading that led to the same kind of imagination and yearning and that he therefore inhabited Emma as well as being half in love with her. But Flaubert was the sorcerer and Emma the sorcerer's apprentice.

Perhaps the same relation holds true for Cervantes and *Don Quixote*, whose early reading got him revved up for his deluded knight-errantry.

When I was fourteen and fifteen I had no inkling of the danger of being overwhelmed. And I wasn't conscious of the apparatus of story, the mechanism and chemistry by which these vapors were condensed by the writer into a book to be reheated and released by the reader. I was interested in the possibility of course. I tried writing a single sentence that might appear on a page of such a book. This was mimicry, abject worship rather than a forthright attempt to assume adult powers.

The other day I saw a television program about child prodigies who play the violin. Most of the adults interviewed said that child prodigies are freaks, that they attract circus spectators, not serious music lovers. A fifteen-year-old violinist with a concert career said that when he plays soccer he's still a kid but that when he plays great music he feels entirely grown up. I thought that this was a touching and dignified answer and probably true. The sample of his playing sounded ffind to me. However, his response reminded me of how uninstructed and unskilled—how unconnected to the adult enterprise of story writing—I was at his age.

But it was at about that age that my reading began to change. Two things happened. One was *The Catcher in the Rye* by J. D. Salinger. The protagonist/narrator is, as I remember, about fourteen or fifteen. He spoke a language that was eerily close to my English at that time. I found out later that Mary McCarthy in her review of the book called it "ventriloquism." She meant that as a sneer. I thought the book was magic. If Holden Caulfield could be the hero of a story, if his experience of psychic bruises was a story, if his language could tell a story, then I wasn't living an unborn life. To book-aided daydreaming I added the seductive thrill of an author setting a good story in my very circumstances. This wasn't Penrod or Tom Sawyer. Holden Caulfield had the shimmer of right now, right here, his inner thoughts closer than those of my roommates'.

The other thing that happened, a counterweight to being a lost boy found, was aspiration. This was still in part the earlier urge to sight the planet that grown-ups lived on, but I began to aspire to be transported to the planet by culture. When I unwrapped the dust jacket of a Modern Library Giant, I found printed inside a list of all the Modern Library books. I thought that if I read all of them I would be transformed more effectively and completely than I would be by, say, doing my homework or by going to confession and taking Communion. Doing homework and being good felt like being held in place. Having friends and playing sports were important, but they were part of my life as it was. (What strikes me as odd now is that although I had some friends who were probably going through this same stage of reading, we never—well, hardly ever—talked about books.)

This ambition was Boy Scout merit badging but also a genuine quest. I was Ponce de León seeking the fountain of age. One bad part was that I was reading books that didn't necessarily have anything to do with each other. It was a long time before I got any sense of the long conversation on a subject that can go on between books—the realization that, for example, Friedrich Nietszche's *The Birth of Tragedy* is arguing with Aristotle's *Poetics*. So there were some books that I slogged through without registering any connections or learning much except vocabulary. But once in a while something stuck. I knew something about the Napoleonic Wars from reading the Captain Horatio Hornblower series in which Napoleon was the enemy. But that was

on a level of boys' games, cops and robbers, cowboys and Indi-
ans. So without any sense of conflict I'd also, from ages eleven to
fourteen, idolized Napoleon, collected lead soldiers of his army,
daydreamed about his devoted marshals Murat and Ney. I'd also
bought at the Paris flea market a bronze commemorative medal
minted in France. It had a profile of Napoleon, the date and
place of his death (5 mai 1821) and the sonorous inscription "*À ses
compagnons de gloire, sa dernière pensée*" (To his companions of—or
perhaps *in*—glory, his last thought). It took me a while to figure
out that Napoleon hadn't actually touched it, but it still gave me
shivers to think that I *held* his last thought. So at age fifteen I
tried *War and Peace*. Tolstoy goes after Napoleon in a way that I
couldn't ignore. On top of that there is a secondary character, a
young cousin of Prince Andrei's, I think, who is boyishly besot-
ted by Tsar Alexander I in the same way I was with Napoleon.

War and Peace had for me the flow of military adventure and
romance that I was used to, but there were contradictory turbu-
lences. Aside from having to come to grips with the folly of hero
worship, I also had no idea what to do about the death of Prince
Andrei or about Natasha's silly infatuation with Anatole, clearly
a bad guy, when she was properly in love with Andrei. I found
myself recognizing details of emotions with which I was familiar,
so precisely described that I attached to them with a number of
minute connections rather than with the easier clichés I was used
to. But sometimes I found these familiar emotions to be shown
up as juvenile or otherwise unsound. Love of glory and falling-in-
love-and-that's-that were only the first two. There was also Pierre,
the apparently unheroic cohero. He is looking for the answers to
the big questions. Answers-to-the-big-questions stuff was familiar
enough, and I could understand his disillusions along the way. I
was even prepared for Pierre's finding the beauty of simple reli-
gious faith from a peasant. That sort of thing came up in the reli-

gious instruction I was taking in with determined piety. (I'd also read Franz Werfel's *Song of Bernadette*.) But that Pierre ends up in the epilogue in middle-age with a half-happiness and a half-faith was horribly unfamiliar and upsetting. I didn't get it. I didn't get it because I was too green. I also didn't get it because the part of it that I *did* get was too dark, too mute, too mournful to contemplate. I thought I either had to believe it or forget it. I had no way of stepping back a step, no perspectives of any kind but those of the story. I couldn't forget it, but I let it recede to that distance at which we know there are people in misery somewhere in the world and yet we can still go to a party.

But I must have forgotten that experience, or at least balanced it with other visions, because I remember saying to someone when I was in my twenties that the really great works of literature are those which can be understood by a bright eleven-year-old. I may have just been trying to start an argument. Or I may have been thinking wistfully of the totality of my belief in the events and moods of *War and Peace* (at fifteen I was still more or less eleven, the onset of adolescence having been postponed by two years of Alpine weather and lots of outdoor sports). Or I may have been thinking that the virgin composure, speculative intelligence, and vulnerability, which are the best parts of being eleven are preserved, or at least regained, when we read. I may also have meant by this glorification of age eleven that the store of adult experience and historical and crucial perspective that we bring to reading fiction as adults are best used only as buttresses to the eager, open-eyed reading we did earlier, when a string of words first made our inner sense flicker open to a story as if it were our dream. Better than a dream because the savor of a story comes from someone else.

That infusion of such a totality of other lives is like the asexual conjugation of spirogyra. The spirogyra is a one-celled organism that reproduces itself like an amoeba by splitting in two. But, unlike an amoeba, it gets together with another spirogyra, and the two penetrate each other and exchange nucleic fluids. At the time I took biology it was supposed that they did this for the purpose of rejuvenation, but I imagined this conjugation as infusion of another life. Were it not for language, we humans would have to wait for such mingling to take effect in our offspring.

A possibly bad part of intense precocious reading is what happened to Jean-Jacques Rousseau. He learned to read at age five or six, and he and his father read to each other every night for a year or so, finishing whatever novel they picked up even if it took until dawn. Rousseau comments in his *Confessions* about this "dangerous method." "I had no idea about things before all the sentiments were known to me. I had conceived of nothing. I had felt everything. These confused emotions that I felt over and over didn't alter the Reason that I didn't yet have; but they formed of me one of another temper, and gave me bizarre and romanesque notions about human life of which experience and reflection have never quite been able to cure me."

Sometime after this orgy of novels from his father's library, Rousseau discovered his grandfather's library, and he read the early eighteenth-century equivalent of the Modern Library, heavily ancient Roman, and he became a precociously ardent citizen.

When I first read this passage, I was seventeen. I recognized the "bizarre and romanesque"—perhaps "romanesque" is better translated as "novelistic." But by sixteen I'd come out of the intense solitary reading I'd been in. I was back in America at a school that prided itself on well-rounded boys. Team sports, of course, but also music. It was mostly ecclesiastical. I sang lots of hymns, plain chant, Mozart's *Te Deum*, Bach's *Christ lag in Todesbonden*, Honegger's *King David*. The Berlioz Requiem was an ecstatic experience, but I was one of three hundred in the assembled choirs, happily singing my lungs out in the bass section, buried behind the trombones, kettledrums, and double basses of the National Symphony.

I remember reading only a few books beyond those required for class work until midway through college. Those few were oddly dated. They come under the heading of exhumed pleasures, the sort of books I found in my grandparents' library or in someone *else's* grandparents' library. They were usually yellowed and dusty. The two I remember with particular pleasure are *Kristin Lavransdatter* by Sigrid Undset and *The Romance of Leonardo da Vinci* by Dmitri Merejkowski. These were throwbacks to early innocent gluttony. By age twenty I was a normal habitual reader.

But there was one more category of reading to come after innocent gluttony, spying on the mysteries of the grown-ups, lost boy found, and climbing into culture. I luckily found consolation. I've been acutely miserable only a few times in my life so far—I mean of the order of "[w]hen . . . in disgrace with fortune and men's eyes." The first time was when I was kicked out of college. I read *Moby-Dick* out loud to myself.

After I got out of law school and passed the DC bar, I decided to try to write fiction. I enrolled in the Iowa Writers' Workshop. The first fall I was there I couldn't get started. I was cold. I was having my heart slowly broken by a splendid woman. I read *Don Quixote*.

Twelve years later a good friend of mine killed himself, my first wife left, and my father died. I read all of Kipling's short stories. One particular dark day I read Alice Munro's *The Beggar Maid*.

There has been only one other year of that sort of sadness and anxiety, during which I reread the seven or eight Shakespeare plays I'd seen.

I think the structure of consolation is this: the book has to be large, strong and true enough to contain grief and yet have enough room for other equally powerful parts of life.

During law school, I again began to read a lot (novels and natural history), and I've been reading at a bright eleven-year-old's pace ever since, but that reading is now more often communal—shared in the same way the Berlioz Requiem was shared. I read with some notion of the other readers in my life, some of them writers, all of them companion sensibilities. But I'm grateful for the circumstance of early solitude.

I've been describing categories of reading, but of course they often collapse into one another. After my friend and mentor Peter Taylor died, I read a half-dozen Anthony Trollope novels, more out of his love of Trollope than my own, finding his appreciation a bond.

Several years after my friend and student Breece Pancake died, I read *Night Comes to the Cumberlands* by Harry M. Caudill, a book Breece had told me to read. Trollope and Caudill were both shared reading and consolation, beyond their generally recognizable virtues.

I'm rarely happily conscious of being a writer. While I'm writing I'm self-forgetful. But I'm happily conscious of being a reader. I'm like my old yellow Labrador retriever, not terrifically bright in the human sense, too impulsive to be always obedient, but with a still-eager heart, and above all a good nose, happy to go zigzagging through a field, sniffing the grass, snuffling into thickets, optimistic that there are always more and more strong scents, more birds to flush and retrieve.

How much larger his life became when he learned to read those texts of his.

How much larger my life became when I learned to read mine.

MENTORS IN GENERAL,

PETER TAYLOR IN PARTICULAR

A dialogue between an ambitious young writer who wants to learn the ropes (and perhaps to pull strings) and an older guy who's bemused. "Of course you should do sensible things to make your way, but there's as much good fortune that's by the way."

I'M GOING to try to be serious before Lola gets here. Actually that's not fair. In a lot of ways Lola is more serious than I am. Certainly more focused. Last week I thought she wanted me to be her mentor. Now I'm pretty sure I was flattering myself.

Mentor. The *American Heritage Dictionary*, the *OED*, and the other *OED—Online Etymology Dictionary*—all mention Mentor, the character in the *Odyssey* who's a friend of Odysseus and who guides Telemachus in his search for his father. Sometimes Athena disguises herself as Mentor and lends a hand. But all three dictionaries reach further back and suggest that a common noun came before Homer's naming a character. If you use Google—"mentor, etymology"—you'll find Indo-European root *men*, "to think"; or Sanskrit *man-tar*, "one who thinks"; or, my favorite: "an agent noun of *mentos* which means intent, purpose, spirit, passion."

> LOLA, THE INTERLOCUTRIX: Hello, hello, sorry I'm
> late. I heard that last bit. Greek, Sanskrit. Come *on*.
> Less ivory tower. More here-and-now.
> I weigh in with the *American Heritage Dictionary*: "The
> word has recently gained currency in the profes-
> sional world, where it is thought a good idea to have
> a mentor, a wise and trusted counselor, guiding
> one's career, preferably in the upper reaches of the
> organization."

But it occurs to me that a mentor in the arts isn't quite the same thing as, for example, a mentor in the CIA, an organization with upper reaches and where career guidance is more practically crucial.

So I don't *need* a mentor?
   Some writers do, some don't. But like that part of college life that is neither lecture notes nor wild oats, a mentor can give you a context for what you're learning, can suggest to you what more you're capable of— but, most of all, a mentor can level out the sine wave of arrogance/helplessness/arrogance/helplessness that is often the initial flight path of a writing career.

Hey, I'm not helpless. I'm not arrogant. I think I just need a muse.
   A muse is trickier. A mentor, a decent mentor, won't trick you. When a muse is being helpful, a mentor steps aside. But when a muse is whimsical, a mentor can keep you from going into a tailspin.

In the Bhagavad Gita, Krishna, in human form, starts off as a mentor, gives advice to Arjuna. But then Arjuna asks Krishna to show what he's like as a god. Krishna shows him the energy of all creation. It's more than Arjuna can bear.

There you go with ancient myths again. Something less mythic. *Rudyard Kipling called his muse a "daemon."*

Okay. Glad to hear you mention an actual writer of prose fiction. Get back to *mentors*. An example of a writer who's a mentor to a young writer like me.

Flaubert took Maupassant under his wing. I've heard that Flaubert set Maupassant a useful exercise. The two of them used to sit at an outdoor cafe, I think in the early evening. Lots of the same people passed by every day. Flaubert had Maupassant write one-sentence descriptions. The next day, if Flaubert picked out the right people, Maupassant got a gold star.

Anton Chekhov helped out Maxim Gorki. Read Chekhov's letters to him.

Samuel Beckett was James Joyce's private secretary. (I don't know what they talked about. I hope it was more artistically useful than the conversation Joyce had with Proust when someone got them together. They talked about their respective health problems.)

So Flaubert had Maupassant do exercises. So a mentor is just like a coach, like a personal trainer?

No. Not just. It's not just straight how-to. Some *things can be taught straightforwardly.* Hunters of the Northern Ice *is a book about the Inuit around Cape Barrow, Alaska—before their life changed with the introduction of rifles, outboard motors, and snowmobiles. There is a description of an older hunter teaching a younger hunter how to find a seal breathing hole in the ice and how to har-*

poon a seal. It is probably word for word what the older hunter was told years before. It is not a seminar. It is not a Socratic dialogue. It is not a dialogue at all. Look, this is how you can see a breathing hole is in use and not an old breathing hole. There are not enough seal holes or seals for practice sessions.

Other skills can be taught with more margin of error, but there is still no question of what error is, in say, canoeing. You either are right side up or not. You either get where you're going or not. The man who taught me how to catch fish—

No, no, no. Enough with wildlife. Get back to mentors. *Writing* mentors.

The first time I got stuck writing—really, really stuck—I ran into a well-meaning friend. He said, "Writer's block? Hey, you don't hear plumbers going around talking about plumber's block."

So he's a mentor . . .

No. I went for a walk with Peter Taylor. My mentor. I moaned a bit. Peter nodded but began to talk about a small, remote farmhouse he'd bought. Peter bought houses. It was his vice. It was a less harmful vice, as he pointed out, than gambling, drinking, or running around with fast women. Peter described the house, nothing in it but a table and chair. He loved the view. "But the best thing," he said, "is that nobody sees me, nobody hears me, nobody knows what I'm doing. After a time, who knows how long, I'll go home and write in the basement."

That's it? That's not much.

Perhaps not. Or perhaps a drop of balm.

Tell one with more of a punch line.

Okay. Peter and I had a mutual friend, a very good poet. The poet wrote a short story. He gave a copy to Peter and me. Peter and

I went for a walk. I said, "It's elegantly written." Peter said, "Oh yes, it's beautifully written." "I don't know what it is," I said, "but something's missing." "Yes," Peter said. "It lacks that low vaudeville cunning."

I guess I did ask for a joke.
It's not just a joke.

It sounds like a joke. You take it seriously?
I take it seriously also. Low vaudeville cunning. It should be on the list with Truth and Beauty.

So what does it mean?
It means, among other things, that you, the writer, should pounce.

Pounce?
Pounce. Have you watched a cat hunt? You know something is going on—the cat gets low and creeps. The tail twitches. The rear end wags and then . . . pounce.

Get back to what the writer does.
After you've pounced, you go back and make sure the reader has a chance to pounce. Making sure of your pounce is the cunning. Making sure the reader gets a chance to pounce is the vaudeville.

And the low?
That's the word that made it sound like a joke. It's also the word that makes you remember the whole thing . . . I had a housemate, a smart, earnest woman, an animal-rights activist, member of PETA. She acquired a beagle. She named it Bagel. I like most dogs. I tried with Bagel. I made a trail of dog biscuits on the lawn and lay down. Bagel got within five feet and then ran back under the porch.

But every day Bagel got one dog biscuit closer. Finally he took one from my hand. Mary-Ann said, "Oh Baggie! You see? I told you he was a nice person just like you."

I said, "Jeez, Mary-Ann. Let's just get him to be a dog," and Mary-Ann said, "You'd be that way too if you'd been abused by an Amish farmer."

I see. Key word *Amish.* The key word is the *pounce.* But can we leave the cats and dogs, the fish, the seals, for God's sake? What is it with you and animals? I don't want to write for *Animal Planet.*

It's not just animals. I wouldn't write fiction if I didn't read a lot. But I also wouldn't write fiction if I didn't spend time bumping into the physical world.

You're certainly easily distracted by it.

I'm easily interested.

Well, right now I'm interested in a practical matter. What about an agent? Isn't an agent a kind of mentor?

Sometimes. But the starting point of that relationship is contractual. It's a business deal, which may or may not include friendship or long-term wise counsel. At the bad end there are sad stories. I've heard that Nelson Algren got fleeced by an agent. At the good end there's Alice Munro and "Ginger" Barber, who used to be Munro's agent. A dozen years ago Alice Munro told Ginger that she, Alice, was all written out, Ginger did not cry out or keel over. She mulled it over in a sympathetic way. After a bit Ginger suggested that she and Alice spend some time together. Ginger's idea was that she and Alice could look over all of Alice's published work with an eye to putting together a book of selected stories.

By the way, Alice Munro's Selected Stories *is a great way to start if you're not already a fan. It begins with some of the lyric*

*single-voiced stories that are like piano or violin sonatas. It moves
on to the more complex dramatic stories that are like string quar-
tets. I wish there were a tape recording of the discussion Ginger
and Alice had. But, perhaps because they know each other so well,
it wouldn't be clear to anyone else. I'm thinking of Ludwig Witt-
genstein's remark: If a lion could speak, we still wouldn't understand him.*

*I don't know how long the discussion went on, but not long
afterward Alice Munro was writing new stories.* Selected Stories
*came out in 1996, dedicated to Ginger Barber, "my essential support
and friend for twenty years."* Queenie *came out in 1999.* Hate-
ship, Friendship, Courtship, Loveship, Marriage *in 2001.*
Runaway *in 2004.* The View from Castle Rock *in 2007.*

*I don't think Ginger was sure it would turn out that way, but
she had an intuitive sense that was better than shrewdness. It was
wholehearted empathy. Here is the part of me that is closest to you.*

That's nice. So how do I find an agent like her?

*Here's what you can do to narrow your search. Find out what
agents represent writers you admire, writers whom you resemble or
hope to resemble.*

*I don't know that many agents—most writers know two: the one
they fired and the one they hired. And most writers don't expect the
Ginger Barber kindredness. They're happy to have a good agent. I
have a very good agent. I'm very fond of my agent. I love our yearly
lunches, but if they were the only meals I ate . . .*

Then what about editors?

*The main job of an agent is to find not just the publishing house
that is good for your work but the editor in that house. That requires
a thick Rolodex and a lot of intuition. It's a hard job—but it's selling to one person at a time. Editors have to think about selling to the*

public. Or to the reading public. Or at least to enough of the reading public to turn a profit.

Once upon a time it may have been that an editor could say to herself, I love this book, and surely there are thirty-seven thousand people like me, and all we need are five good reviews in national newspapers, and Bob's your uncle." Ask an editor if this is the case now and hear him laugh. Or weep. And then he'll say, "If you're a writer, you don't want to know."

It could be that what he doesn't want you to know—leaving aside the input from the publicity department or even the sales staff—is that he's flying blind. He's in a business that doesn't have a business model. There's no brand. You don't hear "Ballantine Books Build Bodies Eight Ways." Each book is its own brand. It's an impossible business.

Editors are torn between loving your work and selling your work—trying to guess *how to sell your work. Sometimes they're telling you to make changes that they think will get them to love your work more, and sometimes they're suggesting changes that they imagine will help it sell more. Sometimes they can't tell the difference. Sometimes* we *can't. It's a mess.*

I'm sorry I asked.

And yet. And yet. My editor is one of the smartest people I know. And unlike some, she really edits. Once we sat side by side at her desk and turned every page of a five-hundred-page manuscript one page at a time.

Although, on the second day, somewhere around page 300 she tapped her finger on a sentence and said, "That line. Were you drunk?"

Was she right?

She has a good ear for bad notes. A line here, a line there—that's okay. When she cuts off a bigger hunk I go into shock. I wish she were more of a believer in cheering the troops on.

"The more we love our friends, the more we criticize them."
Molière said that.

Wrong. Molière wrote that. Alceste says it. Molière is making
fun of Alceste. Alceste is the title character in The Misanthrope.
It is true that of all the title characters Molière makes fun of—the
miser, the would-be gentleman, the affected woman, or Tartuffe, the
pious hypocrite—Alceste is the one you can kind of admire. He's
very smart. His fault is that when he sees a fault in someone else, he
jumps on it. He's right, but he's wrong to be so fiercely right.

You mean he's someone who says things like, "That line. Were
you drunk?"

Yeah.

Or someone who says things like, "Wrong! Molière *wrote* that.
Alceste *says* it."

Oh. I'm sorry.

I hope so . . . So, when your smart editor is pulling your novel
to pieces, do you argue? I'll bet you do—I'll bet you get up in
her face.

No. No—I'm mute. I'm paralyzed. It's back to the lowest part of
the sine wave: helplessness. Then I get depressed for months. Then I
think of arguments. I have arguments with her in my mind. I get her
in the witness box and cross-examine her. In my mind I'm a terror.
"Isn't it true that when I showed you the third rewrite, you said, 'I
don't like X. Get rid of her'? And yet here's the fourth rewrite and
you're saying, 'I like X. I want more of her.' " But arguments, *even*
if you win them, don't help. If someone, if anyone, says, "It's not
there yet. Make it better"—of course she's right, even if the sugges-
tions aren't ones that make it better but just move things sideways.
So you're on your own, and you're paralyzed, depressed, and mut-

tering arguments to yourself that take up all your time and keep you from writing.

So what do you do?

Aside from violent exercise, there are two things that can help. One is to remember that when editors say, "Change X to Y," very often a slight variation of X is all they really want. I've had a couple of experiences of that kind. For example, an editor says, "Page 3 of your fifteen-page story is way too long." You puzzle over it, rewrite two sentences, change the font, and the editor says, "Good." It's actually frightening when that happens. But considering the whirl of manuscripts that is an editor's life, it's not surprising they suffer from amnesia.

And there's another possibility. The most cynical dictum to come out of the school of thought called legal realism is this: law is what the judge had for breakfast.

So what's the second thing to do?

In the case of paralysis, depression, and fruitless anger, get a second opinion. I'm lucky to have a friend, a retired professor of comp. lit., whose taste and judgment I know. We pass books back and forth for each other to read. We've team-taught a couple of courses. We both went to Peter Taylor's memorial service.

Twenty years ago, Tony used to render opinions that were so compressed they were like particles of antimatter he'd found in a black hole. An example: I loved James Salter's Light Years. *I gave it to Tony. Tony's review in its entirety: "Luminously depressing." After he retired, he began to write stories. His son grew up to be a very good fiction writer. Tony's opinions became less terminally adamantine.*

He's read my current manuscript. Another five-hundred pager. He typed an eight-page, single-spaced commentary, chapter by chap-

ter. He had some minor cautions, more notes of satisfactions, one major reservation ("The ending is both too elegiac and too hasty"). But he gets the point of all the characters, gets the coherence of the world they live in. What he conveyed *was: I have considered the matter for all I'm worth and you should get back to work.*

So how do you people find each other? How did Alice Munro find Ginger Barber? Or Gorki find Chekhov? Maupassant find Flaubert?

Affinity.

And that means?

On the same wavelength. First you intuit affinity from a few clues. Then you confirm it by shared reading, shared reactions, shared storytelling. Some people think friendship and even love is based on shared taste. I don't think that's necessarily so. I know lots of people who have friends who share almost none of their tastes. And there are a few people who share tastes but who aren't friends. But it's nice if there's an overlap. It's nice if you can say we share a "final vocabulary." That's a phrase of the philosopher Richard Rorty.

So it was affinity that got Peter Taylor and you together?

Yes. But there was something else. An odd coincidence that started our thirty-year friendship. During my third year of law school I signed up for a writing course Peter Taylor was teaching. In those days you could take an extra course in the arts and sciences. I submitted a novel I'd written during summers when I should have been clerking at a law firm. Our first conference was very short. Peter said, "If I'd known from the beginning that this was a comic novel, I believe I would have laughed a good deal." And then: "You should write some short stories."

After a month or so of writing every weekend from Friday noon until Sunday evening, I turned in two stories. I showed up for our second conference in my army uniform. I said, "I'm sorry. I forgot I had a Reserve meeting. I can't stay long."

Peter said, "This won't take long." I sat down. Peter said, "Don't be a lawyer. You're a writer." I was speechless. Peter said, "We must conspire about this later. As it happens I have to go out too. Some friends are taking me to a party to watch the election returns."

"As it happens . . ."

As it happened, the party Peter's friends were taking him to was the huge party my parents gave every four years on election night—a mix of my father's old political friends and academic acquaintances and a variety of other people whom my mother and a brother of hers knew, and people these people knew. That sort of party. Peter, after a swirl through the crowd, found himself trading stories about Tennessee politics with an equally enthusiastic teller of stories about Massachusetts politics. The Massachusetts man's wife changed the subject long enough to find out that Peter was a writer, spending a semester teaching a fiction writing course at Harvard. "Can you teach writing?" she asked.

"Perhaps all one can do is encourage," Peter said. "Just this afternoon I told a young man, 'Don't be a lawyer, you're a writer.'"

"Yes," my mother said. It was indeed my mother, eager to join Peter in abstract loftiness. "If someone has a talent, he should pursue it no matter what."

As it happened. As it happened, I had finished my Army Reserve meeting, taken the MTA, and at that very moment was making my way through the room. Peter saw me first. He said, "There he is! That's the very young man!"

Every few years after that, either Peter would ask me or I would ask him if it really happened that way. Yes, all the details dovetailed.

So, forget affinity. It was just dumb luck. Without your Peter Taylor you'd be working at some white-shoe law firm.

Possibly. More likely government work. Some years later I told William Maxwell that story and several other less inadvertent instances of Peter's guidance. William Maxwell then sent me one of his habitually short notes—"You are fortunate. Few writers are as generous as Peter Taylor."

So it was dumb luck? You wrote a couple of good stories and you got a godfather. What are the odds? Like getting struck by lightning.

I'd written a pile of stories and a novel. But you're right, it was luck that I found Peter, that he was an encouraging teacher. He was a tutelary spirit.

Tutelary spirit. I had a great-aunt Ida who talked like that. Look—I just want a mentor who's been around the block, someone who looks out for me, someone who writes me recommendations, someone who finds me a job, someone who finds me a publisher. Is that too much to ask?

It's not asking too much; it's not asking enough. The part you want is the way it was with Roman senators and their clients, the way it still is with a lot of politics and business—"Okay, you're a smart kid. Maybe we can help each other out"—a quid pro quo. That's the relationship for people who read neo-Machiavellian how-to books that say things like "Don't make friends, make allies."

Isn't that the real world? Maybe you're living in a dreamworld.

Maybe. Maybe. The editor of the first story I sold was William Maxwell. He was a wonderful writer as well as an editor. I didn't meet him face-to-face until he'd edited three stories. We did it by mail, except for the time he telephoned to ask me to read a paragraph out loud. He wanted to hear if a sentence in it needed a comma. When we finally did meet for lunch, we talked about Joseph Conrad. He'd considered Conrad in detail. After lunch he suggested an experiment in writing that he thought might lead me into a new cycle. He understood how cycles work, and his guess was that I was nearing the end of a cycle. He'd read seven stories and had bought three. This was disinterested advice, as he was about to retire. It was good advice, so carefully offered it was eventually irresistible.

Eventually?

Yes. It took a while to think it over. What I did right away was to reread a lot of Conrad in light of what he said. It's the by-the-way parts—

You really like the by-the-way parts—

Yup. The man who taught me how to catch fish—

You're going there no matter what—

—taught me the first parts in very narrow detail. He was like an Inuit seal hunter. I was living on a four-acre island not far from the mouth of Narragansett Bay. He said, "See those rocks out to the southwest? When the sun gets low, when the bottom part gets orange and when the top half of the tide is running, cast your plug out there." That worked. Next week he said, "See that one big rock to the nor'east? Get yourself some clam worms. Go out in your boat at sunset, top half of a dumping tide. Drop your anchor. Bait your hook. Put a cork on your line an arm's length up. Let your line out about a stone's throw."

I said, "Exactly how far is that?"

He said, "About as far as you can throw a stone."

First you're all Hindu myths. Now you're all quaint New England.
*This instruction went on for a year. We caught striped bass,
bluefish, flounder, fluke, tautog, squeteague—*

I've got the picture.
*No, you don't. Not yet. One evening just as it got dark, he showed
up at the end of the dock in his boat. I said, "I'll get my fishing rod."
He said, "Nope. Just get in." We went out a ways, and he cut
the motor. We drifted in the dark. He said, "Look down there."
What had happened was that the incoming tide had brought in
whole banks of phosphorescent plankton. When something brushed
them, they lit up. It was like looking at an x-ray, a living x-ray of
everything that was going on down there in the salt water. Big fish
made pale green outlines of themselves, then swam off and left dwindling trails of light. An eel made a quick bright wiggle, then vanished. Most likely hid under a ledge. There were other flashes and
shimmerings. I couldn't tell what. That part was as if the northern
lights were in the sea. My point is by the way. Of course a mentor
helps in practical matters, is an adviser. I'm not saying that isn't so.
I'm just saying there is something more important. A mentor points
out things he has seen that are wonderful in themselves. A mentor
points these things out to someone he hopes will go on seeing them.*

Acknowledgments

The following essays were originally published in the following books and periodicals:

"Dogma and Anti-dogma" in *The Writing Life*, Random House (NYC) 1995

"Justice" in *Outside the Law*, Beacon Press (Boston) 1997

"What's Funny" in *Story Quarterly* 39, ed. M.M.M. Hayes, 2003

"Meanwhile Back at the Ranch" in *Sewanee Writers on Writing*, L.S.U. Press, 2000

"Neighbourhoods" in *Unfinished Ireland: Essays on Hubert Butler*, ed. Chris Agee, *Irish Pages* (Belfast) BT 15GB

"Childhood Reading" in *For the Love of Books*, ed. Ronald B. Schwartz, Berkley Books (NYC) 1999

"Mentors in General, Peter Taylor in Particular" in *Mentors, Muses & Monsters*, ed. E. Benedict, Free Press, a division of Simon & Schuster 2009, reprinted in Excelsior Editions, imprint of State University of NY (Albany, NY) 2011

Bibliography

Aristotle. *Poetics.* Translated and with critical notes by S. H. Butcher (1898). New York: Dover Publications, 1951.

———. *The Complete Works of Aristotle,* volume II, Princeton/Bollingen series LXXI.2. *Poetics* translated by Ingram Bywater, 1907.

Babel, Isaac. "A Letter." In *The Collected Stories of Isaac Babel.* New York: W. W. Norton, 2002.

Benedict, Elizabeth. *The Joy of Writing Sex.* New York: Holt Paperbacks, 2002.

Bergson, Henri. *Laughter, An Essay on the Meaning of the Comic.* Translated by Cloudesley Brereton and Fred Rothwell. New York: MacMillan, 1914.

Blok, Aleksandr. *Poems (In Russian).* Create Space Independent Publishing Platform, 2013.

Bowen, Elizabeth. "Her Table Spread." In *The Short Story* by Sean O'Faolain. Old Greenwich, CT: Devin-Adair Publishers, 1983.

Browning, Robert. "My Last Duchess." In *The Poetry of Robert Browning.* New York: W. W. Norton, 2007.

Butler, Hubert. "Peter's Window." In *Escape from the Anthill.* Mullingar Ireland: Lilliput Press, 1985.

———. "The Children of Drancy." In *The Children of Drancy.* Mullingar Ireland: Lilliput Press, 1985.

Chekhov, Anton. "The Lady with the Dog." In *Anton Chekhov Later Short Stories, 1888–1903.* Edited by Shelby Foote. Translated by Constance Garnett. New York: Random House, 1999.

———. "The Lady with the Little Dog." In *Stories of Anton Chekhov.* Translated by Richard Pevear and Larissa Volokhonsky. New York: Bantam, 2000.

Faulkner, William. "Barn Burning." In *Short Story Masterpieces*. Edited by Albert Erskine and Robert Penn Warren. New York: Dell, 1954.

Fitzgerald, F. Scott. *The Great Gatsby*. New York: Scribner, 1925.

Flaubert, Gustave. *Madame Bovary*. Excerpts translated by John Casey.

Foote, Shelby. *Fredericksburg to Meridian*. Vol. 2 of *The Civil War: A Narrative*. New York: Random House First Vintage Books Edition, 1986.

Gibbon, Edward. *The History of the Decline and Fall of the Roman Empire*, vol. 2. London: John Murray, 1862.

Giedion, Siegfried. *Mechanization Takes Command*. New York: W. W. Norton, 1969.

Haley, Alex, and Malcolm X. *Autobiography of Malcolm X: As Told to Alex Haley*. New York: Random House Ballantine Books Group, 1964.

Joyce, James. *Ulysses*. New York: Random House Modern Library, 1934.

Junger, Sebastian. *The Perfect Storm: A True Story of Men Against the Sea*. New York: W. W. Norton, 2009.

Keyes, Daniel. *Flowers for Algernon*. New York: Mariner Books, 2005.

Lawrence, D. H. "The Horse Dealer's Daughter." In *Selected Short Stories*. New York: Penguin Classics, 2007.

Mayhew, Henry. *London Cheaters and Crooks*. London: Folio Society, 1996.

Melville, Herman. *Moby-Dick or, The Whale*. New York: Penguin Books, 2003.

Morris, Desmond. *The Biology of Art*. London: Methuen, 1962.

Nabokov, Vladimir. *Speak, Memory*. New York: Random House First Vintage International Edition, 1989.

Neruda, Pablo. "Bestiario." *Estravagario*. Argentina: Losada, 1900.

O'Connor, Frank. "The Sorcerer's Apprentice." In *Fish for Friday*. London: Pan Books, 1982.

Orwell, George. "Such, Such Were the Joys." In *Essays*. New York: Everyman's Library, 2002.

Orwell, George. *Homage to Catalonia*. London: Mariner Books, 1980.

Poe, Edgar Allan. "The Black Cat." In *Edgar Allan Poe: The Complete Tales and Poems*. Edison, NJ: Castle Books, 2002.

Rousseau, Jean-Jacques. *Confessions*. Excerpts translated by John Casey.

Salter, James. *Light Years*. New York: Random House, 1975.

Scarry, Elaine. *The Body in Pain*. New York: Oxford University Press, 1985.

Shakespeare, William. *Henry V*. In *The Norton Shakespeare*. Edited by Greenblatt, Stephen, Walter Cohen, Jeanne E. Howard, and Katharine Eisaman Maus. W. W. Norton, 2008.

———. *The Merchant of Venice*. In *The Norton Shakespeare*. Edited by Greenblatt, Stephen, Walter Cohen, Jeanne E. Howard, and Katharine Eisaman Maus. W. W. Norton, 2008.

———. *The Tempest*. In *The Norton Shakespeare*. Edited by Greenblatt, Stephen, Walter Cohen, Jeanne E. Howard, and Katharine Eisaman Maus. W. W. Norton, 2008.

Stanislavski, Konstantin. *An Actor Prepares*. New York: Routledge, 1936.

Thomas, Noel Francis and Mark Turner. *Clear and Simple as the Truth*. Princeton: Princeton University Press, 1994.

"Testimony of Oscar Wilde on Cross Examination (April 3, 1895) (Factual Part)," accessed December 11, 2013, law2.umkc.edu/faculty/projects/ftrials/wilde/Wildelibelowfact.html.

Vonnegut, Kurt. *Slaughterhouse-Five*. New York: Dell Mass Market Paperback, 1990.

Wallace, David Foster. "A Supposedly Fun Thing I'll Never Do Again." In *A Supposedly Fun Thing I'll Never Do Again*. New York: First Back Bay, 1998.

Webster, John. *The White Devil*. In *The Duchess of Malfi and Other Plays*. New York: Oxford University Press, 1996.

Wilde, Oscar. *The Importance of Being Earnest*. Mineola, NY: Dover Editions, 1990.

Zola, Émile. *Germinal*. Translated by Roger Pearson. New York: Penguin Classics, 2004.

Permissions